PORSCHE

PORSCHE
ROAD CAR · RACE CAR

ROGER W. HICKS

COURAGE BOOKS

An imprint of
RUNNING PRESS
PHILADELPHIA, PENNSYLVANIA

Canadian representative: General Publishing Co., Ltd.
30 Lesmill Road, Don Mills, Ontario M3B 2T6

9 8 7 6 5 4 3 2 1
Digit on the right indicates the number of this printing.

ISBN 1-56138-001-6

This book was designed and produced by
Quintet Publishing Limited
6, Blundell Street
London N7 9 BH

Creative Director: *Terry Jeavons*
Art Director: *Helen Beauvais*
Designer: *Wayne Blades*
Editor: *Sarah Buckley*

Typeset in Great Britain by Central Southern Typesetters, Eastbourne.
Manufactured in Hong Kong by Regent Publishing Services Limited.
Printed in Hong Kong by Lee Fung Asco Printers Limited

First Published by Courage Books, an imprint of Running Press
125 South Twenty-second Street
Philadelphia, Pennsylvania 19103

C O N T E N T S

INTRODUCTION

PORSCHE: GRAND PRIX DE L'ENDURANCE 1982

ABOVE *The 1982 Le Mans endurance race – darkness falls, but the cars keep up their relentless pace around the circuit.*

T he last thing that was visible in the fading light was the flame that spurted intermittently from the tail-pipes of the Chevvies. The engines roared and spat on the overrun as the cars hurtled past the stands, slowing for the corner. Music that must once have been popular brayed tinnily from the speakers. There was a smell of hot-dogs and fried onions and Algerian *merguez* sausage and beer, mixed with the oil and exhaust and rubber; propped against a wall, drunk as a lord on cheap red wine and surrounded with breadcrumbs, an English motor-racing fan snored noisily. It was the cinquantieme grand prix de l'endurance du Mans; *the greatest sports-car race in the world. In English, it was the 50th Le Mans 24-hour race, and it was destined to become one of the most famous of a famous line.*

It was plain that we were not going to be able to see very much more that night. We spread our sleeping bags on the grass, in the open air, about 50 feet from an earth bank which was the only sound-break between us and the cars;

BELOW *The Belga Team Joest Porsche in the Le Mans pits during the practice.*

and our lullaby was the steadily rising and falling drone of the Porsches.

We had not gone specifically to see the cars from Zuffenhausen, but by now it was clear that they were going to be the stars of the show, as they had been so often before. The Porsche team already bore the numbers 1, 2 and 3. The little 911s were circulating steadily, set fair to win the Index of Efficiency which had by then become almost a Porsche benefit; the 935s, a design already six years old, were well to the fore; and the 956s, with more than 600 horsepower on tap, dominated everything.

We woke with the dawn; the air was cold and there was dew on the grass, but (unlike most years), it had not rained during the night. We made our way back to the stands. By now, the Porsches were even more dominant; we watched with increasing fascination as other cars fell out or made unscheduled stops, and we listened to the same steady drone of the German hovermotor, *the horizontally opposed design that is still, to many, the only permissible layout for a Porsche engine.*

LEFT *The 956 Porsche of Holbert and Haywood (number 3) finished third in this classic Porsche 1st, 2nd, 3rd victory.*

The day wore on. Now, that summer afternoon is long in the past, and the details of who dropped out and who limped home are forgotten; all I can recall is that in that year, no one died on the track that has claimed so many lives. The last few minutes of the race, though, are something I will always remember: as I write these words, the memory brings out the goose bumps on my arms. Precisely, neatly, almost slowly, the 956s arranged themselves in team order: 1, 2, 3. They were no longer racing; they were doing their lap of honour, before *the race was over. And that was the way they ended*

BELOW *The 1928 Mercedes with supercharger, seen passing through Marostica in northern Italy during the 1988 Mille Miglia.*

the race: Jacky Ickx (partnered by Derek Bell) won in Number 1, followed by Number 2 (Mass/Schupan), and then Number 3 (Haywood/Holbert). The 935s that followed them in were almost an anticlimax.

The reason I have dwelled so long on that one race, when there have been so many before and since, is precisely that it was a grand prix de l'endurance; *and endurance is what makes Porsches so fascinating. Not just endurance on the track, or in private hands – one of my closest friends has now put 120,000 miles on his 911SC – but endurance as a concept, as an* engineer's *car which, somehow, has become* everyone's *car; at least, if they can afford one.*

To dwell on Herr Dr. Ing. h.c. Ferdinand Anton Porsche and his achievements is, in a sense, to miss the point of Porsche cars. First, and above all (if you can afford them), they are for driving. A famous French fashion designer is reputed to have said, 'If someone walks into the room wearing a dress that I have designed, and everyone says,

ABOVE *The revolutionary Porsche-Cisitalia race car with four-wheel drive. Lack of funds meant it was never raced, however.*

"What a beautiful dress," I have failed. But if they say, "What a beautiful woman," I have succeeded.' A Porsche gives you a sense of being someone special; you drive as if you have to live up to the car. Your temper improves miraculously; if anyone overtakes you or cuts you up, it is because you have given them permission to do so, or because they are suicidal idiots, not because their cars are more powerful or their driving more skilful. You know *that if you had to, you could lose them as if they were standing still.*

BEFORE THE VOLKSWAGEN 1900–1933

A bove all, Ferdinand Anton Porsche was an engine designer. Throughout his life, he was concerned with making reliable, and preferably very powerful, engines. More often than not, the chassis in which the engine was mounted was not up to the standard of the engine; the handling of many Porsche-designed vehicles, from the Mercedes sports cars of the 1920s through the Auto-Union racers of the 1930s to the Porsche 356 of the 1940s and 1950s, was often terrifying. Even the handling of the seemingly immortal 911 owes more to the skilful 'faking out' of inherent defects than to good basic design. But the engines, ah, the engines . . .

Of course, the Porsche cars we see today are a long way from the designs of the 'Herr Doktor Doktor', who died early in 1951. But no history of Porsche cars could be contemplated which did not also give an account of the man who gave his name to some of the most desirable cars in the world, and founded the dynasty which to this day remains very prominent indeed. And the best way to look at the life of Porsche is to relate it to the engines and the automobiles that he designed. We cannot look at it through his eyes, but at least we can look at the problems which he faced, and we can see how he solved them.

At the beginning of the twentieth century there were already three serious contenders for automobile propulsion systems in the

ABOVE *Ferdinand Anton Porsche, 'Herr Doktor Doktor', in discussion, 1937.*

RIGHT *The 1924 Targa Florio. Ferdinand Porsche, right, talks to Alfred Neubauer.*

running: steam, electricity, and the newer internal combustion engine.

Each had its advantages and its drawbacks. Steam technology was well understood, and there were no tricky clutches or gearboxes to deal with; you just fed steam into the cylinders, and moved away, surprisingly quietly. On the down side, steam automobiles (like steam locomotives) had a prodigious thirst for water; required a more or less lengthy warming-up period, in order to gather sufficient head of steam to drive away; and were occasionally prone to frightening and sometimes dangerous boiler explosions.

Electricity was also well understood. Like the steam car, no clutches or gearboxes were required. In addition, electric vehicles were very clean, and all but silent. Their drawbacks, though, were very high weight (because of all the batteries), very modest speed, and a very short range between recharges: many could only manage 20 or 30 miles, and 50 was good. Of course, you could build faster electric vehicles – in the 1890s, a land speed record of 95 mph was set by an electric car, the *Jamais Contente* – but then your already limited range fell dramatically.

Finally, the internal combustion engine had the potential for immense power and enormous range. It carried its own highly concentrated fuel around with it in a tank which could easily be refilled wherever petroleum spirit was available. It was also subject to the worst disadvantages of any of

ABOVE *The birthplace of Ferdinand Porsche in Maffersdorf, Bohemia.*

the three systems. It was a relatively new technology, and therefore unreliable; it involved a number of complicated parts, such as carburettors and (later) spark plugs with their attendant electrical components; it was noisy, malodorous and dirty; and unlike either steam or electric cars, it needed some means of disengaging the engine from the driven wheels (a clutch). If the full potential of the motor was to be realized, it needed a gearbox as well. Even today, learners have difficulty mastering clutches and gearboxes; in those days, when bicycles and sewing machines were the most complex mechanical devices that most people had encountered, the problems must have been enormous.

By training and inclination, Ferdinand Porsche was an electrician. He was born at Maffersdorf rechts der Neisse, in what is now Czechoslovakia but was then a part of the Austro-Hungarian Empire, on 3 September, 1875. His father was a tinsmith, and he was apprenticed to the same trade. His first encounter with the electric light came in 1890, and by 1892 (when he was 17), he had learned enough to wire his father's house for the new energy source.

Impressed with his son's ability, his father sent him to the *Abteilung Werkmeisterschule* ('Foreman division') of the *Kaiserliche und Konigliche Staatsgewerbeschule für Maschinenbauwesen* (Imperial and Royal

RIGHT *The young Porsche in his father's workshop; he built the machinery himself.*

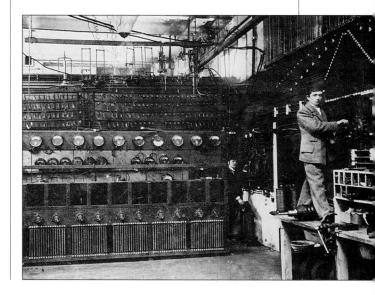

State Trade School for Machine Building') and in 1894, at the age of 19, he left to work for the *Vereinigte Electrizitäts Aktiengesellschaft* or United Electricity Company in Vienna, where he was put to the time-honored apprentice's job of sweeping the floor. By the age of 23 he was *Betreibsleiter* (works-manager) of the experimental shop.

While he was there he designed his first automobile, naturally enough with an electrical drive. In order to lose the bare minimum of power, he positioned the motors at the ends of the axles, where they drove the wheels directly. According to his own later account – which we have no reason to disbelieve – this design was stolen by the boss's son, and the boss, rather than risk a falling-out in the family, told his young employee to forget about it.

Whether he forgot about it or not, young Ferdinand did something about it. He accepted an offer from Ludwig Lohner, the Imperial carriage builder, and went to work for him as an automobile designer. The first Porsche design to be built, the Porsche-Lohner Chaise with its direct-drive hub motors, was one of the stars of the 1900 Universal Exposition in Paris and won a prize. The car was quiet, smooth, reliable, and could cover 80 kilometres or more – say 50 miles – on a single charge.

The range of the new cars was its only limitation, and it was one which Porsche solved with his customary ingenuity. He built a *mixte* drive: an internal combustion engine driving a generator which in turn drove the hub motors.

The result was extremely smooth and easy to handle. The car was an immediate success, and everyone who could afford one (a familiar theme with Porsche designs!) queued up to buy one. Even His Imperial and Royal Highness the Archduke Ferdinand praised the vehicle, in which he was driven by no less a person than Porsche himself, who was a reservist in the Imperial armies. In 1905 Porsche was awarded Austria's Poetting Prize, one of the highest honors that could be

ABOVE *During 1900, Porsche moved to Lohner & Co and installed his wheel-hub motor in one of their vehicles. Exhibited at the Paris World Exposition, it inspired great interest.*

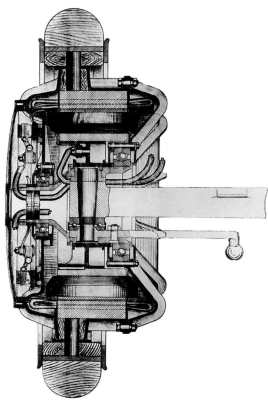

LEFT *A cutaway of the System Lohner-Porsche hub motor.*

bestowed on an engineer, for his contributions to automobile design.

Although the *mixte* drive is now commonly referred to as a dead end, it is worth remembering that diesel-electric locomotives use exactly the same system to this day, for exactly the same reasons: no clutch, no gearbox. *Mixte* drive also has the considerable advantage that any number of wheels can be driven; during World War I, Porsche was to design his extraordinary 'caterpillar' units, in which the front unit carried a generator and all the units behind it were themselves powered from the generator which drove their hub motors. On rough going, the advantages of having every single wheel powered are obvious; the longest 'trains' had something like 48-wheel drive!

Herr Lohner spent a million Austrian crowns on the development of the *mixte* drive, and thought (perhaps understandably) that he could now sit back quietly and sell the 33,000-crown vehicle to all comers. However, his chief designer had more ideas, and more ideas, and more ideas, and when in 1906 an offer came from Austro-Daimler for a position as technical director (with a seat on the board), he could not resist. He was only 31 years old, but he already had the Poetting Prize under his belt, and he apparently parted

RIGHT *The view of the Austro-Daimler factory c1915. Porsche was offered a position in the winning car at the international Prince Henry trials, 1910. Two more 90bhp Austro-Daimlers, designed by Porsche, finished 2nd and 3rd.*

ABOVE *Diagrams of the 1901 Lohner-Porsche Mixtewagen chassis.*

from Lohner on good terms. Very little was heard of Lohner thereafter, though the company went on to manufacture trams and even (after World War II) scooters; but their moment in the spotlight of automotive history was gone.

The next few years were mostly spent refining existing designs. The 1909 Maja (named after one of Emil Jellinek's daughers – a pretty compliment which Daimler Stuttgart also paid to her sister Mercedes) was a 32 hp

four; a heavily modified version of the same car was entered in the Prinz Heinrich Fahrt. This race, named after the Kaiser's brother, was an endurance race which lasted a week, and all three of the Austro-Daimler entries (one driven by Ferdinand himself) put up flawless performances and won silver plaques.

For the 1910 Prince Henry, he fielded an even more radically modified vehicle with 80 bhp, a top speed of 90 mph, and such refinements as cast steel liners (instead of a cast-iron block) and wire wheels instead of wooden artillery wheels. The Porsche-designed Austro-Daimlers came in 1, 2 and 3.

These spacings are not consistently used just as the cars that bore his name would do almost three-quarters of a century later in a race that was not yet conceived: Le Mans. Endurance . . .

Porsche had already designed, and Austro-Daimler had already built, aero engines when World War I came. Aero engine practice cross-fertilized automobile engine design, though automobiles were pushed into the background during World War I. During this otherwise unhappy time, though, Porsche was made *Generaldirektor* of Austro-Daimler in 1916 and received an honorary doctorate (Dr. Ing. h.c.) from Vienna Technical University – quite an accomplishment for a tinsmith whose education had been aimed at nothing more than making a factory foreman out of him!

RIGHT *The 1906 Austro-Daimler Type Maja.*

BELOW *On June 8 1910 Ferdinand Porsche won the Prinz-Heinrich-Fahrt.*

BOTTOM *A 1913 Austro-Daimler six-cylinder engine, installed in both military and civilian aircraft.*

After the defeat and breakup of the Austro-Hungarian Empire in 1918, times were hard; Porsche did little that was remarkable until 1921, when he met Count Sascha Kolowrat at the Brescia track in Italy.

The car he designed as a result of that meeting reflected his delight in small but powerful engines. The 1100cc sohc racer which Porsche designed and built in 1921–22 was called the Sascha, after the Count. It won its class in the 1922 Targa Florio, one of the most demanding races of all time, but unfortunately the success was not repeated at Monza: the cars were unreliable, the pistons burned, and Fritz Kuhn, one of the drivers, was killed. The result was that the racing program fell into bad odour at the plant; and what was more, the *Herren* of the Board did not agree with Porsche's ideas of turning the little Sascha into a 'people's car.' They were more interested in selling to the monied classes, which gives rise to the old joke, 'Und here we see the *Herrenvolk*, the *Herren* in their Mercedes and the *volk* in their wagons.'

Rather more serious than this difference of opinion, though, was the row with the *Osterreichische Kreditanstalt*, the bank that was the majority shareholder in Austro-Daimler. This was the time of hyperinflation, and the bank was pulling the reprehensible trick of holding onto the hard currency that it received for the cars that were sold, and crediting the company's account with the rapidly-depreciating Austrian schilling. This was the era when, it was said, a worker would take his pay home in a wheelbarrow, but his wallet would hold all that he could buy with it. At the crucial board meeting, when the bank refused to credit Austro-Daimler with the hard currency that the company was earning, Porsche told the bankers in colourful terms what he thought of them, stormed out, and never returned.

His talent was such that he did not lack for another offer, this time with the parent company, Daimler, in Stuttgart. He was made technical director, again with a seat on the board, and immediately took over the Indy team: blown 16-valve monoposto fours which, unfortunately, did not receive quite enough development and did poorly at the Brickyard.

Within a year, though, a development of the same basic design was fast enough, strong enough and reliable enough to win the Targa Florio (again!), an achievement which led to Porsche's second honorary doctorate, this time from the Stuttgart Technische Hochschule; he was now known as 'Herr Doktor Doktor' Porsche.

At Daimler, racing had always been a way of improving the breed and advertising the product, so a major victory meant that the board was willing to give Porsche his head. A blown 32-valve straight eight was the immediate result, in which Rudolf Caracciola won the first German Grand Prix to be held after World War I, at the Avus circuit in 1926. Count Zborowski died in a similar vehicle at Monza, but his death was overshadowed by Caracciola's victory, and Porsche's star was in the ascendant.

A few weeks after the Grand Prix, though, Daimler and Benz amalgamated – an event which was to have unfortunate repercussions. Daimler still believed in racing, and allowed Porsche to design an increasingly powerful range of cars: the Benz faction, with more financial clout, was more interested in solid,

ABOVE This 1911 aeroplane also used an Austro-Daimler engine.

BELOW Here, Fritz Kuhn is at the wheel of the triumphant Sascha race car at the 1922 Targa Florio. Porsche can be seen just on the right behind the car.

respectable cars, and fought against the ever more glamourous Mercedes models designed by Porsche.

The flagship of these was the Type 600 straight 6 of 6240cc displacement, with its alloy block and steel liners. The somewhat confusing designation '24/100/140' referred to the 24 fiscal horsepower (worked out on such factors as piston area and number of cylinders); to the 100 horsepower available without the blower; and to the 140 horsepower which was available when the accelerator was floored, which clutched in the blower and provided an extra 40 horsepower in a matter of seconds.

The supercharger was *not* intended for constant use: rather, it was a means of providing the extra power needed for overtaking, or for acceleration to an even faster cruising speed. When the blower was running, the scream of the engine was unearthly; such young bloods as could afford the car were apparently given to flooring the accelerator when passing under railway bridges, just for the sake of the sound! To be sure, the engine was overstressed when the blower was running, but brief periods of overstressing are not harmful to a properly designed engine, and the unblown engine was distinctly understressed and flexible, so the driver had the best of both worlds.

ABOVE *A portrait of Direktor Ferdinand Porsche taken in 1910.*

BELOW *The winner of the 1926 German Grand Prix at the Avus circuit was Rudolf Caracciola, seen here in his Mercedes Benz.*

Such a motor obviously cried out to be installed in a proper sports car, and in 1927, Daimler built the Mercedes K (for *kurz* or 'short', because of the 14-inch reduction in the wheelbase). The power was hair-raising for the day, at 110 unblown or 160 with the blower engaged, but the handling was so bad that the car was popularly called 'the death trap' and the brakes were even more frightening: it took 145 feet to stop from 40 mph!

Fortunately, the K was developed in a matter of months into the S, one of the greatest sports cars of all time. Still powered by a straight 6, this time of 6.8 litres, the power was up to 120/180. There was a new chassis, underslung at the rear axle; and there were massive new brakes, so it would stop as well as go. In June 1927, Caracciola and Rosenberger drove the new cars at the first race at the new Nürnbergering circuit in Germany and devastated the opposition, a legend was born.

Not content with this, Porsche designed still more powerful models: the SS with its magnesium block, 7022cc swept volume and 170/225 horsepower, and the SSK, on a 116 in (290 cm) wheelbase instead of the 134 in (335 cm) of the SS. At the German Grand Prix in 1928, Porsche-designed cars repeated the trick that the Austro-Daimlers had achieved in the Prince Henry in 1910: driven by Caracciola, Merz and Werner, they finished first, second and third. It was becoming a Porsche trademark.

A brief aside is in order here. Different sources give different power outputs for the same cars; for example, the SSK is variously quoted as 140/200, 160/200, 170/220 and 170/225 horsepower. There are two good reasons for this. One is that engines (and dynamometers) vary to some extent, as do methods of measurement. This problem remains to this day, with the distinction between DIN and SAE horsepower confusing matters still further. The second reason for the variations is that there were numerous factory variations in detail and in boost pressure, which led to a fair range of actual power outputs – which, in many cases, may not have been dynamometer tested anyway. One variation, with the *kompressor* permanently engaged, was good for 300 horsepower, this was used in the last and greatest of the series, the Super Sport. Kurz Leicht ('light'), which actually appeared after Porsche left Daimler at the end of 1920, although it was clearly a development of his design.

The reason for his departure was that the Benz fuddy-duddies, eager to oust the old Daimler enthusiasts, engineered a situation in which Porsche was almost certain to lose his temper and storm out. The fact that he was designing successful cars (and trucks – one of his 1928 designs won prizes) was irrelevant. They therefore blamed him for the difficult starting of the 38-hp Stuttgart in cold weather. Porsche pointed out in no uncertain terms that this was a production problem, not a manufacturing problem, tore off his hat, stamped it into the snow, and left (as with Austro-Daimler in 1923) never to return.

Again, he did not lack for offers, including one from Skoda in Czechoslovakia. However, Skoda was too intimately entwined with Daimler for his taste, so he went straight to Steyr, at that time a major independent car manufacturer which was producing more automobiles every year than Austro-Daimler. There, he was responsible for the 100 horsepower straight-8 Austria, the hit of the Paris Auto Show in 1929; the same city, of

course, where he had been a star 29 years earlier, at the 1900 Universal Exposition. Again, endurance . . .

Everything seemed perfect, but what he did not know was that Steyr was in deep financial trouble. Worse still, when the crunch came, the company ended up under the control of those same bankers that he had left, with a shouted obscenity and a hurled cigarette lighter, in 1923. Unsurprisingly, they refused to renew his contract. He was 54 years old, and out in the cold.

Rather than trying to fit in with another manufacturer, he decided to set up his own design consultancy studio. Stuttgart was close enough to the centre of the German automobile industry, that it seemed a natural choice; and so, in April 1931, he opened the *Porsche Konstruktionburo für Motoren-Fahrzeug-, Luftfahrzeug- und*

Wasserfahrzeugbau. His partners were Anton Piech, his son-in-law, and Adolf Rosenberger. They owned 15 per cent each of the company, while Porsche kept the other 70 per cent. Others on the team included chief designer Karl Rabe, Karl Frölich (gearboxes), Josef Kales (engines), Erwin Kommenda (bodies), Josef Zahradnik (axles, springs and steering), and Josef Mickl, an aerodynamycist

BELOW This 1929 Mercedes Benz SSK Drop-head coupe has a six-cylinder engine.

and theoretician. Ferry Porsche, Ferdinand's 21-year-old son, was also a member of the firm. With two Karls, the Josefs and two Ferdinands, life must sometimes have been interesting.

Their first commission was a 2-litre car for Wanderer, one of the four companies that merged shortly thereafter to form the Auto-Union (the others were Horch, Audi and DKW). In order not to make it look as if it was the first commission, though, it was arbitrarily numbered Type 7; by which reckoning a 356 is really a 349, but we get ahead of ourselves. The Type 7 went into production, and did very well, though it was not a particularly exciting or interesting car.

Other commissions followed thick and fast. Many were for experimental ideas which never made production status; Porsche's firm served as an experimental shop for a number of manufacturers. One of the most prophetic was the Type 12, which was a prototype low-cost car for Zündapp, the motorcycle manufacturer who could see that automobiles

ABOVE The finish of the German Grand Prix sports cars race at the Nürnbergring, 1928.

RIGHT Karl Rabe was chief designer for the Porsche Konstruktion Buro, which opened in April 1931.

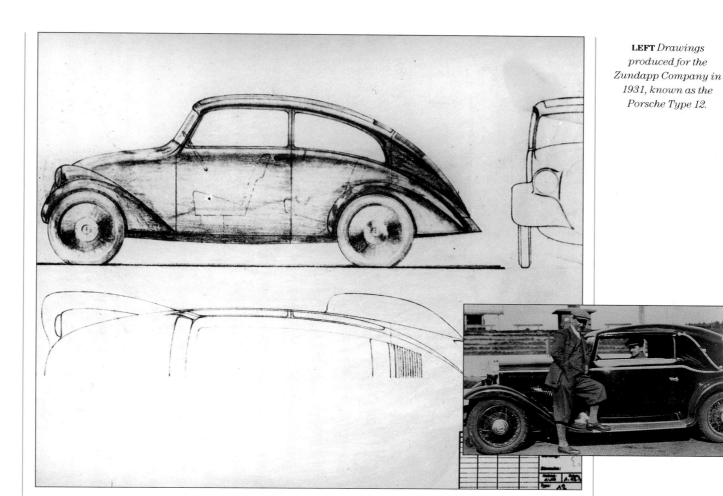

LEFT *Drawings produced for the Zundapp Company in 1931, known as the Porsche Type 12.*

would, sooner or later, replace two-wheelers as the transport of the common man. Although Fritz Neumeyer was enthusiastic, he decided that the investment was too great: he paid Porsche off with 85,000 marks and one of the cars, which was used for a company runabout until it was destroyed in 1944.

With the exception of the engine, which was (rather improbably) a 5-cylinder radial, the Type 12 foreshadowed the Volkswagen, with its four-wheel independent suspension and streamlined body. A little later, the Type 32 was a commission for another motorcycle manufacturer, NSU. Again it came to nothing, again because of the investment required to go into production (about 10,000,000 marks), but it was another step nearer the Volkswagen; a flat four, still mounted at the back, with independent torsion-bar suspension. Air cooling was chosen for both the radial and the four, for simplicity, reliability, ease of maintenance and starting in very cold weather, and (allegedly) for better

cooling on mountain roads. The specifications also called for indefinite cruising ability at what was (for then) the very respectable speed of 90 kph (56 mph) to take advantage of the autobahns which had been coming into increasing use in Germany since the 1920s.

In the meanwhile, the Herr Doktor Doktor was made an altogether extraordinary offer by the Soviet government. In the summer of 1932, Porsche set out on an all-expenses-paid tour of Moscow, Kiev, Stalingrad, Kursk, Nijni-Novgorod, Leningrad, Odessa and the Caspian Sea. At the end of all this, he was asked to consider moving himself, his family and his entire staff to the Soviet Union, where he would be given a blank cheque. As Porsche himself said, 'Well, one isn't supposed to say it, but what I saw was wonderful'. The catch, though, was that he would have to sever all ties with his homeland. Porsche decided that he was too old to do that, so he declined. There was plenty to do at home . . .

ABOVE *The Wanderer W22 cabriolet, 1933. In the car is Ferry Porsche, son of Ferdinand Porsche.*

VOLKSWAGEN AND AUTO UNION 1933–1948

'I have met you before, *Herr Doktor* Porsche!' These were the words with which the Führer greeted the designer in May 1933; that Hitler should have been impressed with the engineer, rather than vice versa, perhaps sums up the difference between the two men.

They had first met (actually, they were merely introduced by Daimler's press agent) at the Solitude Rennbahn in 1924, when Hitler was an obscure local politician. Now, Hitler was the Chancellor of Germany; and he was very keen to get so prominent a designer, now running his own independent design studio, to design both racing cars and a people's car – a Volkswagen – foɪ the Third Reich.

BELOW *The Führer, Adolf Hitler, inspecting the KdF-Wagen at the Volkswagen Werk, May 1938. Ferdinand Porsche can be seen standing beside the car.*

It was not that Porsche was a political man. Indeed, it was the very opposite. He wanted nothing more than an opportunity to work at his beloved projects – and if the new Chancellor was willing to fund this, fine. Porsche's objections to the Soviet Union had not been ideological; rather, they had been the practical precautions of a man who is at home among his own people, who speak the same language and eat the same food. On Hitler's side, though, having an internationally known designer 'on his side' could not but boost his claims that the new Germany really was a forward-looking meritocracy. Also, who would not take the chance to work with a man he had admired for decades, as Hitler had admired Porsche?

It was in May of 1933 that Hitler met Porsche for the second time. The Führer wanted to use motor racing as a symbol of Germany's technological resurgency, and he had already agreed to give Daimler-Benz a subsidy equivalent to $250,000 (£140,000) to develop such a vehicle. Klaus von Oertzen, on the Auto-Union board, believed that with Porsche's help, they could create an even better vehicle; and so he persuaded the designer to come along to meet the Führer.

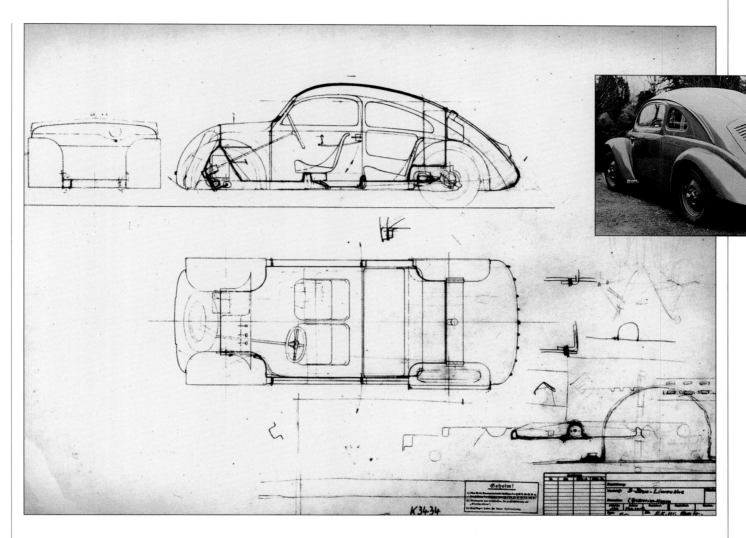

Not only did they get the subsidy but Hitler, the leader of National Socialism, also believed in a 'people's car', and it was on this level as much as on the racing level that he and Porsche saw eye to eye. They were also, of course, fellow small-town Austrians. Hitler's speech at the 1934 Berlin Motor Show clearly showed his commitment to a *kleinauto* ('small car') or even *volkswagen* ('people's car'). Hitler said:

'So long as the automobile remains only a means of transportation for especially privileged circles, it is with bitter feelings that we see millions of honest, hard working, and capable fellowmen whose opportunities in life are already limited, cut off from the use of a vehicle which would be a special source of yet unknown happiness to them, particularly on Sundays and holidays. One must have the courage to grasp this problem in a decided and comprehensive manner. What will not be possible in one year will, perhaps, prove to be a commonplace fact ten years hence.'

Between them, in early 1934, Porsche and Hitler hammered out their idea of a people's car: a four-seater, with a 1-litre engine, capable of cruising at 100 kph (62 mph), with a fuel economy of 7 litres per 100 km (approximately 40 mpg). Porsche worked out that he could do this for M1550, with a car weighing 650 Kg (1430 lb) and propelled by 26 bhp from a low-stressed, long-stroke engine. He asked to be paid for development expenses and then to receive a royalty on each car made.

The wider German automobile industry was opposed to Hitler's ideas about a people's car because at best it did not see any profit in it, and at worst it could forsee spending large sums of money with no return whatsoever, chasing the Führer's impossible dream. Many of Hitler's dreams would soon turn into nightmares, but the Volkswagen was not one of them. Porsche shared that dream, and he was not averse to showing the rest of the German automobile industry that it could be realized.

Unfortunately, for political reasons, Hitler was not willing to accept Porsche's M1550 price, the car would have to retail for M990, below the critical M1000 mark which represented the maximum that many Germans might be able to afford. Worse, Porsche was given only 10 months to develop the car. The *Reichsverband der Deutschen Automobilindustrie* (RDA), under whose auspices the project was placed, must have felt that their reservations were more than justified, and in an attempt to make sure that the project died a quiet but decent death, they cut the budget for development costs to a mere M200,000; but Porsche took the money on the grounds that at least it was a start, and more might be forthcoming later. With nowhere else to work, Porsche's team started to build the car in the garage at his home in Stuttgart in 1934.

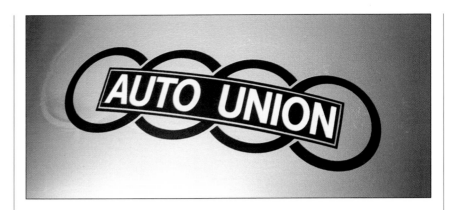

The 10-month deadline was a joke; both Hitler and Porsche soon realized that. In the end, the project also cost over M4,000,000. But Hitler believed in Porsche, and as long as a project had Hitler's backing in Nazi Germany it would continue. By 1936, Porsche decided to go to the United States to see how cars were built there; at that time, of course, American popular cars were the cynosure of the world. By October 1936, 16 months late, three prototypes were made available to the RDA for testing.

No doubt to the chagrin of those gentlemen, whose testing was clearly

ABOVE *A logo from the 1938 D Type GP car.*

RIGHT *The poster opposite reads 'Five marks per week will buy you this car …'*

BELOW *During the 1930s, Auto-Union, aided by the Nazi Party, developed their cars into world beaters. Shown here is the 1938 D Type V12.*

designed to break the little motor cars, they were forced to conclude that the design was 'generally satisfactory' and several more prototypes were built in 1937. Faced with the possibility that a *volksauto* just might be possible, several manufacturers tried to jump into the race they had spurned for four years; at the 1937 Berlin Auto Show, when Opel presented their P4 (at M1450) as a 'Volkswagen', the Führer was incensed, and left the Opel stand without saying another word. And when they suggested that they could make the car at a subsidy of M200 per car, Hitler did some swift mental arithmetic. He wanted to build a million cars: this meant a M200,000,000 subsidy, which would end up in the pockets of the established manufacturers. For the same money, he could build an automobile factory. The Volkswagen, built by the people, for the people, half-a-century before Harley Davidson tried to appropriate the same slogan was born.

The Volkswagen may be the most obvious precursor of the Porsche, but throughout the 1930s, the *Herr Doktor* was also building – and racing, and winning with – some of the fastest racing machinery of all time. His

original meeting with the Führer had secured the $250,000 ($140,000) grant that Auto Union wanted; and the cars that Porsche designed were awesome.

They were all basically similar. The rules called for a maximum weight of 750 kg (1650 lb) excluding fuel, water, driver and (perhaps surprisingly) tyres. The idea of the weight limit was to reduce engine size and speed, but Porsche had several ideas on getting lots of

power from relatively modestly-sized engines. The 1934 models extracted 295 bhp from a 4.5 litre supercharged V-16, an engine which would (with steadily increasing capacity, ending up at 6 litres) eventually be persuaded to yield about 600 bhp. Given that a modern full-dress touring *motorcycle* can easily hit 1000 lb (450 kg), it is not hard to see that the power-to-weight ratio of these P-cars was staggering: better than 600 bhp/ton on the road, complete with fluids, tires and driver.

Power alone was not enough. The cars were also mid-engined, for a number of

LEFT *The 1938 D Type Auto-Union GT car.*

ABOVE *The rear view of the V16 version. This C Type used a 6006cc engine which could reach over 200mph (320kph).*

reasons. One was reduced frontal area: the driver pretty much defined the aerodynamic cross-section of the P-series. Another was weight distribution: a low polar moment of inertia grows steadily more desirable as you increase power-to-weight ratios, though when you do lose control of a well-balanced car with the weight in the middle, you will be going very quickly indeed and you will need to be something of a superman to get it back on

course. Again, the rearward mounting of the engine saved on transmission weight and complexity – though it has to be said that Daimler-Benz achieved similar power-to-weight ratios with more conventional designs.

Only a very few drivers ever tamed the mighty Auto Unions, among them Rudolf Caracciola, Hans Stuck and Bernd Rosemeyer; Rosemeyer himself was killed in 1938 when attempting a speed run on the autobahn. He was travelling at something between 440 and 450 kph (close to 270 mph) when either a

ABOVE *A cutaway view of the 1937 Porsche Type 22-engined Auto-Union racer.*
LEFT *Bernd Rosemeyer, considered by many to be the greatest driver of his time and seen here driving one of the Auto-Union's cars to victory in 1936. Rosemeyer won five out of the six major competitions that year.*

BELOW *A view of the Porsche Type 60, VW test series number 38.*

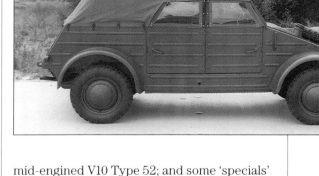

It was easy to adapt the Volkswagen to war use. As the engine was rear-mounted, it was ideal for fitting with a propeller which could be pulled up for land use. Over 50,000 examples of this amphibious schwimmwagen were produced in both covered and open (top left and bottom) versions. The Type 82 Kubelwagen is shown right.

gust of wind or a blow-out caused the car to skid for 80 yards, somersault twice, then fly for 200 yards through the air. Rosemeyer was hurled out during the flight, slammed into an embankment, and died instantly. Porsche was devastated by the death of his 27-year-old protegé, and rarely attended a race thereafter.

Although the Auto Unions were out of the mainstream of Porsche road cars, the mid-engined layout would appear again and again on racers, and even on a few road cars; no lessons that the Porsche design studios learned were ever forgotten. Other projects included the Type 52, a three-abreast sports car (like a modern Bagheera), powered with a development of the Auto Union engine; the

mid-engined V10 Type 52; and some 'specials' based on the Volkswagen, to which we should now return.

The Wolfsburg plant was what we would now call a 'green-field' development. It was to consist not only of a factory but it would also be a city for 100,000 people. On Ascension Thursday, 26 May, 1939, Adolf Hitler himself laid the foundation stone of the factory. However, before a single Volkswagen could be built there, Germany would be at war, and the factory would be turned over to production of military variants of the Beetle, such as the *Kubelwagen* and the amphibious *Schwimmwagen*; the few Volkswagens which were actually built (just over 200) were

virtually handmade in Stuttgart as show-piece models.

The Volkswagen is too well known to need much description, but it is worth remembering that the earliest models had mechanical (cable operated – not hydraulic) brakes; provision for starting with a crank-handle as well as a self-starter; a single combined brake/stop light; and a 30 bhp, 1131 cc engine, which was driven through a 'crash' (non-synchromesh) gearbox. All of these features would also appear on the earliest Type 356 cars.

There were, however, a couple of Volkswagen 'specials' which prefigured the 356 even more closely than the basic *Kraft durch Freude*-Wagen (Strength through Joy, or KdF). There was the Type 64, with an aluminium body on a VW floor pan, and there was 60K10.

The 60K10 was built for a race which never took place, on the *Autobahns* and *autostrade* of the Rome-Berlin Axis. The Volkswagen flat four was enlarged to 1500cc and 'massaged' to give 50 bhp, and the body was a hand-beaten aluminium affair of surpassing smoothness, designed primarily for high-speed cruising. Interior accommodation was tight – the passenger seat even had to be staggered backwards to make room for two people – but there is no doubt that if you look at each part of the car separately there is something about it that is always Porsche. It is only when you look at the vehicle as a whole that it becomes a familiarly bulbous 1930s design; the whole is somehow less than the sum of the parts.

When the war ended, Wolfsburg – like the rest of Germany – was in ruins. During the war Porsche had helped to design munitions like the Elefant tank, as well as civilian-use projects such as wind-powered generators (Types 135, 136 and 137) and basic, simple tractors (Types 110, 111, 112, 113). He had also interceded on behalf of French workers at Peugeot, which was under German management during the war, when they had been threatened by the SS; and although he was given honorary SS rank, he refused to fill

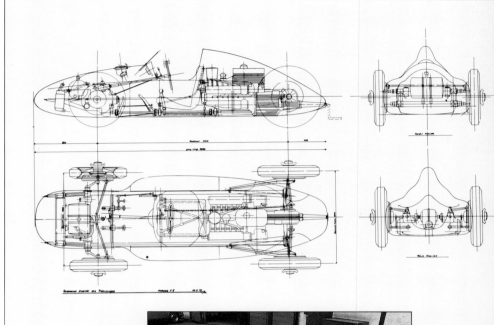

ABOVE *Technical drawing of the Porsche Type 360.*

INSET AND LEFT *The 1960 Type 360 Cisitalia Grand Prix car probably represented one of the most advanced race car developments of its time.*

LEFT *The Cisitalia car was produced in the early postwar years under the supervision of Ferry Porsche and chief designer Karl Rabe. It used a 12-cylinder opposed-piston engine with four-wheel drive. The engine was mounted just behind the single driver's seat.*

in the application papers or even to be measured for a uniform. Perhaps 'refused' is too strong a word; whether diplomatically or genuinely he never found the time to meet the SS tailor who waited for days to measure him up for his uniform.

He was by now an honorary Professor at the Stuttgart Technische Hochschule; he was *Herr Professor Doktor Doktor*, a title which any well brought up Austrian might well employ in full. He was based at Gmünd in Austria, away from the bombs that were falling on Stuttgart, when the Allies entered Germany. He was briefly detained and investigated to see if he was guilty of any war crimes, but he was rapidly freed.

In a disgraceful piece of political chicanery, the Professor was now invited by France to build a French Volkswagen and then (it seems) framed by French automobile makers with the twin purposes of averting potential competition and distracting attention from their own questionable records as collaborators. He was far from a young man at 70, and the conditions in which he was kept after his arrest in 1946 were disgraceful; for the last few months, from early 1947 to late July, he was kept in an unheated dungeon in Dijon, Burgundy.

This is no place, however, to mull over French duplicity that is decades in the past. Suffice it to say that he was eventually freed on half a million francs' bail, which was never returned despite the fact that a French court acquitted him of all charges. He returned to Germany in August 1947; the money that freed him was earned by the Porsche Design Studio, now effectively headed by the Professor's son Ferry, for designing a racing car for Cisitalia.

PORSCHE RESEARCH AND PRODUCTION TODAY

From the first Volkswagen Beetles, designed and developed in the 1930s, through the 356 series to the latest 911 models, Porsche has remained at the forefront of automotive engineering excellence. By combining traditional engineering craftsmanship with state-of-the-art production and design facilities at Weissach and Zuffenhausen, Porsche looks set to maintain pole position for a long time to come.

ABOVE *The main Weissach development centre where prototypes, test engines and transmissions are designed and tested by over 500 specialists.*

BELOW *Complex computer-aided manufacturing (CAM) facilitates the precisely-measured production of experimental parts.*

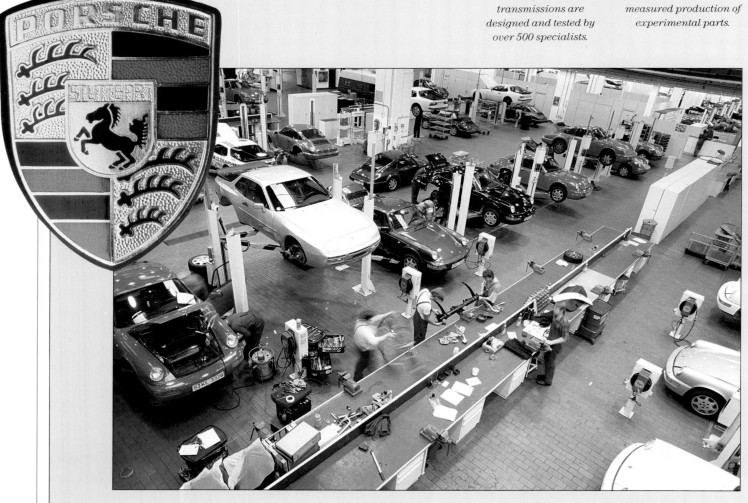

ABOVE *Exhaust tests at Weissach assure adherence to ever more stringent governmental and international emissions legislation.*

RIGHT *Extreme temperature and humidity conditions are recreated in climate chambers such as this, acting as a precursor to testing in frozen Scandinavian wastelands and parched Arizona deserts.*

ABOVE *Improved aerodynamics and lift-free bodies are made possible by prolonged testing in wind tunnels.*

Anechoic chambers localize noise sources and enable accurate analysis of noise levels and frequencies.

Potential passenger injury is investigated by thorough crash testing. The procedure is recorded by sensors and captured by high-speed cameras.

TOP LEFT *A carefully applied coat of paint would not survive the ravages of weather and accidents were it not for the preceding pre-cleaning, rust-proofing and spraying process.*

LEFT, AND OPPOSITE TOP RIGHT AND NEAR RIGHT *The assembly line at Zuffenhausen showcases the state-of-the-art in electronic data processing and factory automation, although each car is still individually constructed.*

ABOVE *Built in 1938, the current Porsche Administrative Offices in Stuttgart originally housed development and production operations. It was here that the Volkswagen was developed to production maturity.*

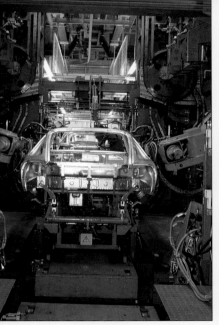

RIGHT *Another Porsche body exits the paint booth; the last coat gives the car its ultimate appearance.*

356

The supercharged flat-12 Cisitalia bore the factory type number 360; but before he had started work on that project, Ferry had also started work on a Volkswagen-based sports/touring car, the Type 356.

As originally conceived (the 356/1), the car was much more radical than the production models. The chassis was a tubular space frame, and the engine was rotated about the rear axle so that it lay between the driver and the rear wheels; it was, in fact, a mid-engined car. The 1131cc Volkswagen engine was given bigger inlet valves to improve breathing – the original design had deliberately been restricted in the interests of longevity – and the compression ratio was raised from 5.8:1 to 7.0:1. With the addition of twin carburettors

instead of the single, tiny stock item, it produced 40 bhp. In years to come, even Volkswagen Beetles would have much, much more than that; but for now it would do. On the nose of the hand-beaten alloy open body,

BELOW *1948 saw the Porsche No 1, Type 356, produced under the direction of Ferry Porsche.*

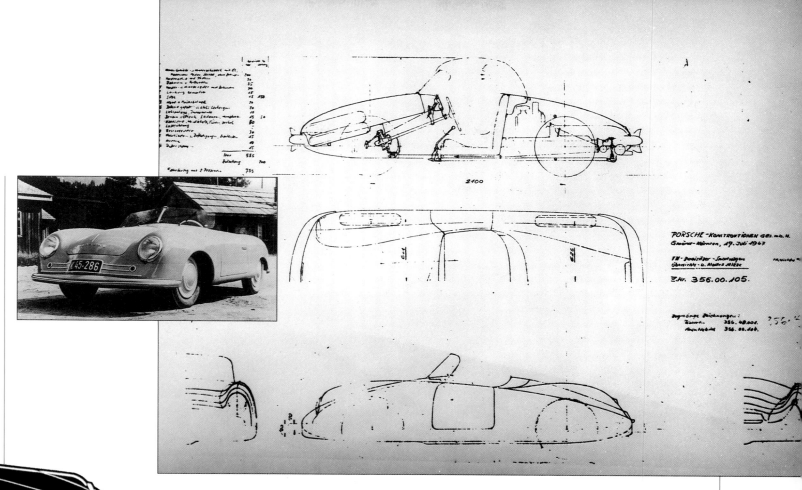

ABOVE *First design drawings for the Porsche 356.*

INSET *The 1948 Porsche Type 356 at the Gmünd works. This is the roadster version.*

ABOVE *A brochure illustration for the 356 cabriolet.*

T E C H N I C A L S P E C I F I C A T I O N	
MODEL	356 1950–7
ENGINE	4-cylinder, horizontally opposed pushrod 1086cc to 1488cc
WHEELBASE	2100mm (82.7 in)
LENGTH	3870mm (152.4 in) pre-52, 3950mm (155.5 in) post-52
WEIGHT	770 to 840 Kg (1694 to 1848 lb)
HORSEPOWER	40 (1100) to 70 (1500S)
ACCELERATION	ca 0–60 mph (96 kph) 16 secs to 13 secs
TOP SPEED	ca 95 to 110 mph (152 to 176 kph)

in the script that is used to this day, it said PORSCHE.

It had much to commend it, but from a production engineer's point of view, it was a nightmare: hand-beaten alloy and space frames were definitely *not* suited to series production. Also, the rear suspension (which was simply Volkswagen suspension reversed) put unacceptably high loadings at the very end of the chassis and led to a weird toe-out attitude in cornering. These disadvantages, rather than the lack of luggage space, were what prompted the 356/2.

Like the Volkswagen, the 356 needs little introduction. It is surely one of the most readily identifiable motor vehicles in the world but the original 356/2 was still some way from the classic 356 models that most of us would recognize today.

The body was still hand-beaten aluminium, though in deference to the European climate it was now a fixed-head coupé. There were opening quarterlights, the rear treatment was very bare, without overriders or a multiplicity of lights. There was a very small glass area: glass is heavy, expensive stuff which most automobile designers would prefer to be without. The windshield was a two-piece 'vee' of flat sheets, very much like the 60K10. The brakes were still cable operated, there was a 4-speed 'crash' (non-synchromesh) gearbox, and the engine breathed through two Solex 26 VFJ carburetors. The rear shock absorbers (dampers) were lever-type, though there were tubular strut shockers at the front. For reasons now completely forgotten, the windshield wipers on the earliest models parked in the upright position.

On the other hand, the steel floor pan with its welded central 'box' spine for strength was already there, and the family resemblance to the cars which would follow for the next decade and a half was unmistakable. Under the skin, there was the Volkswagen-type torsion bar suspension, independent on all four wheels. On the strength of the 356/2 prototype alone, a Swiss dealer ordered 50 of the new cars. The only significant difference between the prototype 356/2 and the production models was the adoption of curved, fixed quarterlights.

LEFT *The Gmünd factory, with work being carried out on a Type 356/2 Gmünd coupe.*

BELOW *A 356A 1600 S coupe of 1956.*

They were built at Gmünd, very, very slowly. In 1948, they made four; in 1949, 25 and in 1950, a mere 18. It soon became apparent that Ferry's original estimates of selling maybe 500 cars, perhaps over a period of several years, was excessively conservative.

Some of the cars were shipped to Switzerland in chassis form; Beutler built six of the eight Cabriolet (drophead) bodies that were built around Gmünd 356/2s. The engine was the faithful 75 × 64mm Volkswagen, though in order to fit inside the 1100cc class for racing, many – perhaps most – of the Gmünd cars were of 73.5mm bore instead of the full 75mm for a swept volume of 1,086 cc. Compression ratios varied, with 6.5:1 a popular compromise between power and the ability to digest low-grade fuel.

In order to expand production, Dr. Ing.h.c. F. Porsche KG ordered 500 bodies from Reutter in Stuttgart late in 1949, to be delivered at a rate of eight or nine a month. The main difference between the Reutter-bodied cars and the Gmünd vehicles was the adoption of flat glass quarterlights and a curved (but still two-piece) windshield. The first cars were delivered in early 1950; by the end of the year, 289 had been sold. In September a birthday party was held to honour the old man; the car park was full of Volkswagens and Porsches. In October, two Porsches were exhibited at the Paris Auto Show: Half-a-century had passed since the young man from Maffersdorf had first stolen the show with his electric chaise, and the banner on the Porsche stand said simply:

1900 PORSCHE 1950

Sadly, just after this show, the Direktor suffered a stroke, from which he never fully recovered. He died on 30 January, 1951, less than two months before the five hundredth German-built Porsche rolled off the production line.

The 1951 Porsches already exhibited the evolutionary tendency which was eventually to separate them almost completely from their Volkswagen roots. The brakes followed Volkswagen practice in changing from mechanical to hydraulic, but they were a twin-leading shoe design instead of one leading, one trailing. Extra power was sought first by boring the engine to 80mm, to give 1286cc and 44 bhp at 4200 rpm, and then towards the end of the year by increasing the stroke by 10mm. In 1952, extra 'stop' was added to the extra 'go', with brake drums which grew from 230mm to 280mm (9 in to 11 in) in diameter and from 30mm to 40mm (1.25 in to 1.5 in) in width. In the same year, synchromesh made the car easier and more fun to drive (despite complaints from purists), and the windshield became a one-piece unit.

However the only way to get the extra engine capacity, was to use a roller-bearing

TOP The 356B had a very different nose to the A. The familiar 'Porschenose' changed to a much prettier American bow with high-mounted bumpers and large overiders. Headlights were raised and pointed blinkers were added.

ABOVE This is the mark of the Reutter Company, purchased by Porsche in the 1960s and which used to make 356 bodies.

bottom end with a built-up crankshaft. While this is perfectly normal motorcycle practice, and tends to produce a 'rev-happy' engine, the only reason for doing it at Porsche was that otherwise the rod bolts at the big end would contact the crank case.

The two absolutely critical things with a roller-bearing crankshaft are frequent oil changes, and not 'lugging' the engine (driving at too-low engine speeds). If you were careful, and lucky – or if you raced the car – the roller-bearing engines were extraordinarily reliable. For the careless and unlucky drivers expensive bottom-end rebuilds became almost commonplace.

head coupé was the standard, though in 1952 there were 16 'America' lightweight roadsters (of which 14 actually got to the United States, where they were raced very successfully), and in September 1954 came the 'Speedster' with its stripped-down roadster body, rudimentary windshield, and hood which seemed to have been designed more to keep the rain out of a parked car than for driving: visibility, headroom, and weatherproofing were all negligible when you were on the move.

This is one of the most desirable of all early Porsches, and demonstrates clearly that beauty is in the eye of the beholder. Many refer to it as an 'ugly duckling' and give it such names as 'the bathtub', but others see it as a wondrous classic, a driving machine without

Gestern noch ein Zukunftstraum …

Der Speedster ist sozusagen das Sonntagskind der internationalen Automobiltechnik. Er ist leichter als Coupé und Cabriolet, noch rassiger in seiner Linienführung und für sonnige Tage der Wagen, den sich alle Glückspilze wünschen. Will man ihn genauer charakterisieren, so könnte man ihn den klassischen Sportwagen der großen europäischen Schule nennen. Der Form nach ist er der Traumwagen von morgen. Pantherhaft geduckt – als könnte er jeden Augenblick zu einem machtvollen Sprung ansetzen – steht er da. Die Straßenlage ist so ideal, daß man auch bei Spitzengeschwindigkeiten nie das Gefühl der Sicherheit verliert. Der Fahrersitz befindet sich genau im Schwerpunkt. Der Heckmotor ist – wie bei den andern Porsche-Wagen – luftgekühlt. Professor Porsche hat seinen ersten luftgekühlten Motor schon 1912 gebaut. Kein Wunder also, daß in den Porsche-Motoren zahlreiche Erkenntnisse und Erfahrungen verwirklicht wurden, die vor allem der Lebensdauer des Motors zugute kommen.

Alle Instrumente befinden sich zentralisiert unter einem Abdeckschirm unmittelbar vor dem Lenkrad (Drehzahlmesser, Tachometer, Öltemperaturanzeige); auf der rechten Seite befinden sich zwei Zierstreifen mit dem PORSCHE-Schriftzug und ein Haltegriff. Die Sitze sind schmaler und leichter als bei Coupé oder Cabriolet 356 und ähneln eher den Sitzen im Rennsportwagen, Typ 550.

Porsche also embarked upon a course of offering a remarkable range of engines. By 1954, you could buy no fewer than six, including an 1100 (1086cc, 40 bhp) with the 73.5 × 64 engine; a 1300 (1286cc, 44 bhp) with the increased 80mm bore; a 1300S (1290cc, 60 bhp), with the roller-bearing crankshaft and a 74.5mm bore; a 1300A (like the 1300S but with only 44 bhp); a 1500 (1488cc, 55 bhp); and a 1500S (1488cc, 70 bhp), both the 1500 models having the 74mm stroke with an 80mm bore. Of this bewildering selection, power-hungry Americans were offered only the 1500 and 1500S.

As it became clear that the 356 was a volume-production car, the bodies also became increasingly standardized. The fixed-

TECHNISCHE DATEN

Motor	1500	1500 S (Super)
Bauart	4-Zylinder-Boxer-Motor, luftgekühlt	4-Zylinder-Boxer-Motor, luftgekühlt
Zylinder-Bohrung	80 mm	80 mm
Kolbenhub	74 mm	74 mm
Hubraum	1488 cm³	1488 cm³
Leistung	55 PS bei 4400 U/min.	70 PS bei 5000 U/min.
Höchstgeschwindigkeit	155 km/h	170 km/h
Kraftstoff-Normverbrauch	7,4 Ltr./100 km	7,9 Ltr./100 km
Fahrgestell	**1500**	**1500 S (Super)**
Länge	3950 mm	3950 mm
Breite	1660 mm	1660 mm
Höhe (mit Verdeck)	1220 mm	1220 mm
Änderungen vorbehalten		

DR.-ING. h. c. F. PORSCHE K.-G. · STUTTGART-ZUFFENHAUSEN

Printed in Germany · 15 M · 6. 55 Gl.

any concessions to ornament or superfluity. It was available only in the United States, which has been the destination of something like half of all the Porsches ever made.

By now opinions were beginning to polarize about the Porsche. One camp held that it was a beautifully made, very quick little motor car which was a joy to drive. The other maintained that this was only true up to a point, and that once you reached that point it was a vicious and tail-happy little beast that would turn around and bite you. The Porsche-can-do-no-wrong school countered that if you knew how to drive, the handling was all but perfect; and the response to that was that if you really knew how to drive, instead of pussyfooting around in the thing, you would

OPPOSITE The Speedstar appeared in 1956, a pure two-seater with fully collapsible all-weather top and a very low, curved windscreen. Today it is a collector's dream.

BELOW The great classic which appeared in 1960 – the 356B Super 90 roadster. New suspension meant a far better ride.

find out just what 'tail-happy' meant, and in a big way. The debate continues to this day.

By 1955, Porsche evidently felt that they had a different enough car to warrant calling it a 356A for the American 1956 model year. The windshield was now curved smoothly, instead of being essentially a one-piece copy of the old two-piece screen with a 'fold' in the glass in the middle; the wheels shrank in diameter from 400mm to 375mm (16 in to 15 in), but grew in width from 80mm to 110mm (3.25 in to 4.5 in), allowing the use of 5.60 tyres instead of 5.00; and there was, once again, more power.

The old 1100cc engine disappeared, and the baseline became the 44 bhp 1300 plain-bearing engine; except that now, the bore was the 74mm of the formerly roller-bearing type, and the stroke was 74.5mm. The 1300S, still with roller bearings but of the same bore and stroke as the plain-bearing engine, offered no less than 60 bhp at 5500 rpm, aided principally by the availability of better fuel: the compression ratio was up to 8.2:1 from the 'cooking' 6.5:1. Both of these options were, however, dropped for the 1958 model year, and the 1600 became the bottom model.

Perhaps surprisingly, plain bearings reappeared in the 1600cc capacity, achieved with a new crank case, cast-iron cylinders and

TECHNICAL SPECIFICATION	
MODEL	356A 1955–59
ENGINE	4-cylinder, horizontally opposed pushrod, 1582cc; double overhead cam 1498cc and 1588cc
WHEELBASE	2100mm (82.7 in)
LENGTH	3950mm (155.5 in)
WEIGHT	815 to 950 Kg (1793 to 2090 lb)
HORSEPOWER	44 (1300) to 115 (Carrera 1600 GS GT))
ACCELERATION	0–60 mph (96 kph) 12.8 secs to 10.1 secs (Carrera)
TOP SPEED	102 to 121 mph (163 to 193 kph)

TECHNICAL SPECIFICATION	
MODEL	356B 1959–63
ENGINE	4-cylinder, horizontally opposed 1582cc to 1966cc
WHEELBASE	2100mm (82.7 in)
LENGTH	3950mm (155.5 in)
WEIGHT	875 to 1040 Kg (1925 to 2288 lb – Carrera heaviest)
HORSEPOWER	60 (1600) to 130 (Carrera 2000)
ACCELERATION	0–60 mph (96 kph) 13.5 secs to 11.5 secs
TOP SPEED	109 mph (174 kph) (average)

ABOVE A sporting highpoint in the life of the 356 range was the Carrera GTL-Abarth. It was a lightened GT car assembled by Carlo Abarth of Turin. Between 1961 and 1963 it was powerful enough to win the world championship for GT cars up to 2000cc.

a new bore of 82.5mm. The old 74mm stroke was, however, retained for a displacement of 1582cc. In 'Normal' guise (also known as 'Damen' or 'Ladies" model – oh sexist days) the 1600 delivered 60 bhp at 4500 rpm with a compression ratio of 7.5:1, while the 1600S offered 75 bhp with a compression ratio of 8.5:1. The early 1600S (until September 1957) had a roller-bearing bottom end, but the later models were once more plain-bearing.

There was, however, still one roller-bearing engine; and fearsome it was. With four overhead cams, twin-plugged cylinders (much needed with a 9.0:1 compression ratio!) and dry-sump lubrication, it was essentially a down-rated version of the 550 Spyder racing engine (see Chapter 7). It delivered 100 bhp at 6,200 rpm, and it was about 100 lb heavier

than the pushrod models with a front/rear weight distribution of 41/59. This was more than enough to get the driver into deep trouble unless he or she spent several months learning how to drive an essentially overpowered and very tail-happy car.

This was the first 'Carrera', and in 1957 the ultimate roadgoing Porsche was a Carrera Speedster. It abounded with 'added lightness' including lighter bumpers and plastic windows, and even the heater was removed to reduce the weight. The only things that were heavier were the wide 60mm (2.3 in) brake drums at the front, much needed to control the kind of speed of which the car was capable. The all-up weight was little more than three-quarters of a ton, and the power of all the Carrera engines was increased 10 per cent to 110 bhp at 6400 rpm, so the acceleration was electrifying. If you were content to drive normally, the recommended rev range was 2500 to 6500, but the engine would accept full throttle from 1500 rpm and would run to 7500 rpm if it had to. Even if you were going slowly, you could always admire the 160 mph speedometer and the 8000 rpm rev counter! For 1958, the same power was retained, but the engine reverted to the less temperamental plain-bearing design.

For those who liked the wind in their hair, but found the Speedster a little too basic, there was also a Cabriolet with a higher windshield, a proper padded hood which (like most German hoods) did not really fold away properly, and rather more creature comforts such as roll-up windows. The Speedster, of course, was intended for Southern California where even the natives (in the teeth of the evidence) forget that it does sometimes rain.

Despite the obsequious style of reporting which was normal in the motoring press in those days; despite the golden haze which tends to surround one's memories of classic cars in their heyday; despite the fact that the 356A, with its longer, thinner rear torsion bars and fewer-leaved front torsion bars was a much smoother car than the 356; despite all this, it still had its flaws. The handling was a little better, thanks to the process of 'faking out' which had already begun, but the throttle linkages (which were exceptionally long and complex) would sometimes disintegrate; the clutch cables used to break, just as they do on motorcycles; and the oil cooler had a habit of developing leaks, which meant major investigative surgery before you could even see the thing. Of course, with the kind of power that the newer engines delivered, 'air cooled' was something of a misnomer: like all subsequent 'air-cooled' Porsches, the engines in these are liquid-cooled, except that the liquid in question is oil rather than water and antifreeze. The Carrera, in fact, had *two* oil coolers.

Another 'problem', unique to the American market, was the spartan interior trim of Porsches: bare metal and rubber floor mats were something that surprised some Americans, a problem which survives to this day; where else would you find a motoring correspondent complaining about the lack of a radio in a Ferrari F40, or about the fact that the doors had light, fast, efficient wire pull-openers instead of door handles? That actually happened in California in 1990! For those who wanted speed and luxury in their Porsche, the 1959 3560/1600GS offered 105 bhp at 6400 rpm, but weighed 2,100 lb.

The trouble was, though, that this kind of obesity (svelte though it may have looked next to the American land barges of the day) was making the Carrera uncompetitive, and Porsche wanted a sports-racer. What they did, therefore, was to contract with Zagato (through Carlo Abarth) for a series of lightened Carreras, called (predictably) the Abarth Carrera GTL; the first of these appeared in 1960.

Everything was lightened, with even the hub-caps made of light alloy, and light alloy doors and hood and trunk lids. The bumpers were lighter, there was less interior trim, and the engine rose steadily from 115 bhp at 6500 rpm to 135 bhp at no less than 7400 rpm.

BELOW A 1956 Carrera GS seen at the 1988 Mille Miglia. The name 'Carrera' was to be applied in memory of an endurance race in Mexico; the cars that carried it were to become some of the fastest road cars in the Porsche line-up.

ABOVE *The 1956 356C was the last of the line, after 76,303 356s had been produced.*

T E C H N I C A L S P E C I F I C A T I O N	
MODEL	356C 1963–65
ENGINE	4-cylinder, horizontally opposed 1582cc to 1966cc
WHEELBASE	2100mm (82.7 in)
LENGTH	3950mm (155.5 in)
WEIGHT	935 to 1040 Kg (2057 to 2288 lb – Carrera heaviest)
HORSEPOWER	75 (1600) to 130 (Carrera 2000)
ACCELERATION	0–60 mph (96 kph) 13.2 secs to 11.5 secs
TOP SPEED	109 to 115 mph (174 to 184 kph)

OPPOSITE *The 10,000th Porsche, about to be driven away by Ferry Porsche on March 16, 1956.*

BELOW *The Porsche badge seen on the hub cap of the 356 SC.*

To return to the mainstream, though, the 356B made its appearance in 1961, and it was a much more modern looking car, with a foretaste of the 911. The headlamps were raised considerably, so that very little painted metal appeared above them: the bumpers were enlarged and raised, probably in acknowledgement of the traditional American way of parking; and air intakes for brake cooling appeared just behind the bumper.

The brakes were still drum, but they were radially-finned Alfins, and the top-of-the-line engine (short of the Carrera) was the Super 90, a development of the 1600S engine with a 9:1 compression ratio and (what else?) 90 bhp at 5500 rpm. At the rear of the car, a transverse leaf spring was added, while the torsion bars were reduced from 24mm to 23mm to reduce rear roll stiffness; another example of the progressive improvements made to both ride and handling, but which were still essentially a way of 'faking out' the problems associated with rear-engined cars.

For many people, the definitive 356B was the 1962 model (first shown at Frankfurt in September 1961), with its significantly larger glass area; it made the old cars look surprisingly old-fashioned overnight. This was also the year when the Carrera 2 was introduced, the 356B version of the Carrera, and this was where things got really hairy.

The long-suffering double-knocker flat 4 was redesigned yet again with a 92mm bore and a 74mm stroke, for 1966cc – effectively, 2 litres. In a well-streamlined car that weighed under 2000 lb (900 kg), 130 bhp led to truly spectacular performance; in the United States, similar power was regarded as more than adequate for hauling cars that were 50 per cent heavier. The top speed was published as 125 mph, but Porsche (like their compatriots BMW) has always been among the few firms which is conservative about top speed; 130 mph or more was fairly readily available, and in the proverbial situation of 'down hill with a following wind', 140 mph was not impossible.

ABOVE *A brochure for the 356 cabriolet.*

slip under full acceleration. But then, it was not built as a dragster; it was built as a car to drive at high speed, and at high speed it could most assuredly be driven.

This was the last of the 356 Carreras, though there was an even more impressive racing version which could be driven on the road, the 2000 GS GT with 155 horsepower; but that properly belongs in Chapter 7.

By now, the Type 356 was nearing the end of its life. The original 356 had lasted from 1948 to 1955–6; the 356A from 1955 to 1959/ 60; and the 356 from 1959 to 1963. The last Type 356, the 356C, entered production in July 1963 – Porsche never cared much for the American 'model year' system – and lasted for about 26 months.

It was, however, the greatest of the 356 series in the eyes of most; in the words of one enthusiast, 'you get more of the better Porsche qualities and fewer of the poorer qualities'. The main difference was the adoption of disc brakes all round, plus (of course) still more power: 75 bhp at 5200 rpm out of the 1600C and 95 bhp at 5800 rpm out of the 1600SC, with its higher compression ratio. It was also available with the Carrera 2-litre engine for those who wanted it. A great to-do was made by some motoring journalists about the deletion of the camber compensator (it was still available as a $30 (£16) option if you wanted to order it when you ordered the car). Otherwise, there was little but praise, especially for the new engine which used cast-iron liners cast into a light-alloy finned barrel.

In September 1965, the last 356C was made. In 15 years, between 1948 and 1963, the 356 had progressed from a handmade prototype (and later, a handmade motor car) with a 40 hp Volkswagen engine to one of the most desirable sports cars on the road, powered by engines which were anything from about twice as powerful to almost four times as powerful as the original. The 'Herr Professor Doktor Doktor' whose name the cars bore had passed away, but the company – and the tradition – that he founded were more vigorous than ever.

A unique Porsche design of disc brake slowed the whole plot down when necessary.

It had something of a thirst for oil, it was true, and it was not much of a dragster: the clutch would give up the unequal struggle and

4 911

Ferdinand had designed the Volkswagen; Ferry had designed the 356; and in 1959, Ferry's son 'Butzi' (his real name is Ferdinand, too) started work on a new project, the 901, which was to replace the 356.

They wanted a family resemblance to the 356, but the car could be a little bigger (the wheelbase could be up to 100mm longer, about four inches), and it was expected to be smoother, quieter, more comfortable and more spacious than the 356. Oh, yes; it was also to be more powerful.

In September 1963 – a little after the 356C had been introduced – the 901 was displayed at the Frankfurt Motor Show. The wheelbase was very slightly longer than the target 2200mm (86.6 in) at 2211mm (87.04 in), and the whole car was longer than the 356SC by 153mm (6 in); but the car was, unmistakably, a Porsche. The steering was altogether cleverer, with a ZF rack and pinion; the brakes were of course discs all round; the electrics were 12-volt instead of the dismal old 6v; and the engine; ah, the engine . . .

The four-cam flat 4 had been considered, and then dismissed on the grounds of expense and complexity. Instead, a completely new departure was planned: a flat 6. It was still oil-cooled, but it had a single chain-driven overhead cam for each bank of three cylinders, and dry-sump lubrication. In keeping with modern thinking and the potential for high revs, the engine was strongly oversquare, with an 80mm bore and 66mm stroke. The forged one-piece crank ran in eight bearings, and delivered (in its initial form) no less than 130 bhp at 6100 rpm from

its 1991 cubic centimetres; the same as the old Carrera.

The power was fed to the rear wheels through an all-new 5-speed gearbox, the gate layout of which occasioned some controversy. Second to fifth were in a conventional 'H' gate, with first down and to the left. Americans in

ABOVE *The task of designing a newcomer to the Porsche line-up was left to Ferdinand Porsche 111, better known as 'Butzi'.*

particular seemed to find this too difficult to use, as they viewed fifth (where it existed at all, which was nowhere much in the early 1960s) as an overdrive gear which one would engage for cruising on the freeway and then forget about. First, on the other hand, had to be in line with second for fast, 'drag-racing' type starts.

The alternative view, which has much to commend it in a competition-oriented vehicle, is that you spend very little time in first gear: once the car is rolling, you are unlikely to need it again. At high speed, you are much more likely to be swapping cogs in the third-fourth-fifth range, and a 'dog-leg' fifth with first to fourth in the 'H', and fifth up and to the right, is much less satisfactory.

From a weight point of view, the new car pretty much split the difference between the old 356SC (than which it was about 45 kg (100 lb) heavier) and the Carrera convertible (than which it was about 23 kg [50 lb] lighter), so there was virtually no loss of performance, and the performance was sparkling. There are significant differences in reported weights from different sources, though, so it seems that American models had already succumbed to the general tendency to have more weight (and often, especially in later years, less power) than their European counterparts. Tyre sizes went up to 185/70 VR 15, so there was a little more rubber to get the power onto the deck.

Inevitably the new car was greeted in some quarters with howls of anguish, simply because it was not a 356. It also had a whole new set of handling and other problems which, like the shortcomings of the Type 356, would be gradually 'faked out' over the years. One of the most extraordinary expedients, adopted to counter complaints of a very light front end, was an official factory modification which consisted of bolting cast-iron weights of 11 kg (24 lb) inside both ends of the front bumper – an official variation of the old trick of putting a sack of cement in the front trunk to improve front/rear weight distribution, at the expense of increased polar moment of inertia. The carburation was not particularly clever, either, with severe 'flat spots' from the floatless Solex carburettors and plug fouling in traffic. In February 1966, Webers were used, which improved matters somewhat but still left 'flat spots' which were finally overcome with adjustable accelerator pump rods.

Before the 901 took to the road, though, it was re-christened the 911, for the most prosaic of reasons: in France, Peugeot had copyrighted all combinations of 3-digit numbers with a zero in the middle. As long as cars with such model numbers were not produced in large numbers, like the Bristol 401 to 409, or Porsche's own 904, they were not too worried; but with a new Porsche, which would probably sell very well, they were more concerned.

BELOW Produced in 1961-2, the Porsche Type 695 was a four-seater prototype which looked more and more like the 911.

RIGHT The 911 six-cylinder engine, introduced by Ferry Porsche in 1963, is still going strong in updated versions today.

And sell well it did. Porsche could not produce the new car fast enough to keep up with demand after it went into production in late 1964. Not until 1965 was a right-hand-drive version offered for those who drive on the proper side of the road, and the car hardly changed at all for the first couple of years except for small, detail improvements. Rather surprisingly, Porsche reverted to a four-speed box in the middle of 1965, retaining the five-speed as an option. For many years thereafter, five-speeds sold so well in many markets that they became the *de facto* standard (and they were all that was offered on the faster models), but Americans retained a perverse taste for the four-speed box. In a country where bends are at a premium and average speeds (to say nothing of speed limits) are to European eyes laughably low, this is perhaps understandable.

Also in 1965, Porsche introduced a strange new body style, a cross between a coupé and a convertible. A big, meaty roll-bar was a sort of 'roof'. Behind it, the rear window could be zipped out, and on top (between the roll-bar and the windshield), the roof could be unclipped and lifted off. It was not quite as good as a convertible, but those were the days

TECHNICAL SPECIFICATION	
MODEL	911 1964–71
ENGINE	6-cylinder, horizontally opposed, overhead cam 1991cc to 2195cc
WHEELBASE	2211mm (87 in) pre-1968; 2268mm (89.3 in) post-1968
LENGTH	4163mm (163.9 in)
WEIGHT	1085 to 1125 Kg (2387 to 2475 lb)
HORSEPOWER	110 (911T) to 180 (911S)
ACCELERATION	0–62 mph (99 kph) 8.8 secs to 6.8 secs
TOP SPEED	132 to 140 mph (211 to 224 kph)

when Naderism had ceased to be entirely rational, and the 'safety' hysteria convinced many manufacturers that convertibles would never be permitted again in their biggest single market, the United States. 'Safety' is in quotation marks because anyone who has driven both a Porsche and an American 'land barge' of the mid-1960s will know that it doesn't matter how many air-bags or safety belts or crush zones or acres of metal the manufacturers surround you with, you are just less likely to hit anything in a small, light, nimble, sweet-handling car with good brakes than you are to come to grief in a Naderized behemoth. It's the difference between

LEFT *The dashboard of the 1967 911S.*

secondary safety, or surviving an accident, and primary safety, or not having the accident in the first place.

For the 1967 model year, though, the old, familiar process began all over again: MORE POWER. In July 1966, the engine was given a hotter cam, bigger valves, freer breathing, and Weber 40 IDS carbs; the resulting 911S offered 160 bhp at 6600 rpm: four times the power of the original 1131cc 356. To make life still more fun, the Fuchs five-spoke alloy wheels which are now almost a Porsche trademark were introduced at a weight saving of five pounds per wheel, and unsprung weight at that, the handling improved significantly. An anti-roll bar was added at the back, the brake discs were vented, and Koni shockers became standard. Americans were denied the new engine because of emission controls, but it was very well received in Europe.

There were also four other variations on the 911 in 1967–68, namely the Sportomatic, the 911R, the 911T and the 911S. The Sportomatic was not so much a model as a transmission variation, but selecting this highly undesirable option completely changed (not to say ruined) the car. It was a strange

and rather unpleasant form of semi-automatic transmission with a hydraulic torque converter and a clutch. Built into the gear-lever was a microswitch which disengaged the clutch via a vacuum mechanism and allowed conventional shifting without the need for conventional clutch control. If you unthinkingly rested your hand on the gear lever you also lost all power and made the

ABOVE *The 911/912 Targa, which was introduced at the Frankfurt Motor Show in 1965. It used a built-in rollbar, a removable fold-up roof panel, and on earlier models the rear window was made of plastic and could be unzipped and removed.*

engine scream like a banshee. It was not fun.

It was also excessively complicated: and when it failed, tracking the fault through the electrical, hydraulic and vacuum systems was extremely time consuming. Anyway, because it was still a 'stick shift', it did not appeal to the American public at whom it was aimed. Few people ever had the misfortune to own this mechanical-electrical-hydro-pneumatic abortion, and even fewer have anything good to say for it. I had one; it was unspeakable.

The 911R was another matter. Even fewer people experienced these, which were lightened 911s with racing engines. The sheet metal was thinner, plastic and light alloy were used extensively, trim was reduced, and the whole thing weighed under 900 kg (2000 lb) – maybe 10 per cent lighter than the standard vehicle. This would have been good, but a 10.3:1 compression ratio, 46mm Webers and a general 'breathing-on' of the engine gave it 210 bhp at 8000 rpm. At this point we are up to five and a quarter times the power of the original 356 in a vehicle which weighed less than 50 per cent more! Only 20 of these vehicles were made.

The 911T was at the other end of the spectrum, a lower-powered Porsche with 'only' 110 bhp and a number of economies such as cast iron instead of light alloy

cylinders, solid steel instead of vented brake rotors, steel wheels instead of alloy, and cast-iron instead of steel rocker arms.

Finally, the 911S was a regular 130 bhp 911 engine in the fancy 911S body with the light wheels and better trim. It was mainly for the American market, which had a very rough time with Porsche for a while because of unrealistic emission control regulations which

ABOVE *The dash of the 911S.*

forced engines to run much too lean so that they habitually backfired and misbehaved.

Although the 911T was the 'economy' 6, there was in fact a still more economical Porsche, the 912, which was introduced just a few months after the 911, in April 1965. This was essentially a 911 body with the old Super 90 four-cylinder engine from the 356, and it seems to have been made mainly to provide a transition model between the 356 and the considerably more expensive 911.

With the 95 bhp engine from the 356SC slightly downrated to 90 bhp, it was still good for 115 mph, and the front/rear weight distribution was considerably better than the six at 44/56 instead of 41/59.

OPPOSITE *1967 models of the 911 S had large wheel openings to compensate for the extra width on the brakes. The S also had wider wheels (an extra 6 in) which meant a better ride and handling.*

BELOW *The 911/912 1968 Targa.*

It shared more than the body with the 911, though: for example, 12-volt electrics, a choice of 4-speed or 5-speed gearboxes, multispeed wipers and more. If you compared it with a 356, it was a very fine car indeed; but it definitely suffered in most people's eyes by comparison with the 911, which had almost 50 per cent more power. It was (and is) also noisier and rougher than the 6, and most people who have owned them are quite frank about the fact that they are 'second best': the Porsche for a driver who cannot afford a 911.

Despite this, the 912 ran from 1965 to 1969 and sold over 30,000 cars; indeed, in the first year, the 912 outsold the 911, at 6440 to 4865. It was only dropped to make way for the 'VolksPorsche' 914, and when that experiment proved not to be a success, it was actually brought back (as the 912E) for the 1976 model year, with a 1971cc fuel-injected Volkswagen flat-4 (out of the 411 Variant) delivering 90 bhp. The 912E is not as quick as the original 912, partly because of a weight increase of no less than 270 kg (600 lb) and

Note: Performance figures exclude 'sportmatic' and G11R figures as being outside of the general range.

TECHNICAL SPECIFICATION	
MODEL	912 1965–77
ENGINE	4-cylinder, horizontally opposed 1582cc and 1971cc (1975–77)
WHEELBASE	2211mm (87 in) pre-1968; 2268mm (89.3 in) 1968–69; 2271mm (89.4 in) 1975–77
LENGTH	4163mm (163.9 in) to 1969; 4291mm (168.9 in) 1975–77
WEIGHT	995 Kg (2189 lb) to 1969; 1160 Kg (2552 lb) 1975–77
HORSEPOWER	90 (to 1969) 87 (1975–77) US export only
ACCELERATION	0–60 mph (96 kph) 11.4 secs to 9.7 secs
TOP SPEED	115 to 117 mph (184 to 187 kph)

partly because of increased bodywork drag, but it is still good for 110 mph and is arguably an ideal car for the United States, where it considerably reduces your chances of getting a ticket for speeding.

In August 1968 (1969 model year), a new B-series 911 was introduced with a wheelbase longer by only 57 mm (2.25 in), achieved by lengthening the rear trailing arms. The result was a much better ride, together with a slight

RIGHT *The powerhouse of the 1969 911S.*

ABOVE *Three views of the 1969 911S.*

but significant improvement in front/rear weight distribution, from 41.5/58.5 to 43/57 (per cent), which was aided and abetted by putting the batteries in the front of the car. The rims got wider, to a full six inches, and a slight flare was added to the wheel-arches. On the Targa, the zip-out rear window (which had always been leaky and noisy, and which few bothered to zip out anyway) was replaced with a fixed wraparound rear window.

Perhaps confusingly, though, the new model was not called a 911B; instead, the models were the 911T (now introduced to the American market for the first time), the 911, the 911E (replacing the 911L) and the 911S. Predictably, the 911E gained a few horsepower (up to 140 at 6500 rpm), while the 911S jumped to 170 bhp at 6800 rpm. Both models owed their extra power to the adoption of Bosch mechanical fuel injection, the first time that this was used on roadgoing Porsches.

From then on, the story was one of ever-increasing power, together with almost equally frequent increases in swept volume. Weight also crept up, as it always does, but fortunately not at the same rate as the power increased.

The C-series, introduced in September 1969, were bored to 84 mm for 2195cc, and bigger clutches were fitted to handle the extra power: 125 bhp at 5800 rpm for the 'cooking' 911T, only a little less than the original 911; 155 at 6200 rpm for the 911E; and 180 bhp at 6500 rpm for the 911S. The front upper strut attachment points were moved forward 14 mm (just over half an inch) to lighten steering effort and reduce 'kick-back' through the wheel.

Late 1971 saw a longer bore at 70.4 mm for 2341cc (though the cars were called 2.4 litres). Compression ratios were lowered to

BELOW *With its very familiar RS-style tail, this is the 1973 911 Carrera RS 2.7. Initially 500 were built, followed by 1,000 more in 1973.*

T E C H N I C A L S P E C I F I C A T I O N	
MODEL	911 1971–77
ENGINE	6-cylinder, horizontally opposed 2195cc to 2994cc
WHEELBASE	2271mm (89.4 in)
LENGTH	4147mm (163.3 in) pre-1973; 4291mm (168.9 in) post-1973
WEIGHT	1110 to 1135 Kg (2442 to 2497 lb)
HORSEPOWER	130 to 210 bhp
ACCELERATION	0–60 mph (96 kph) 7.3 secs to 6.1 secs
TOP SPEED	137 to 142 mph (219 to 227 kph) (Carrera 150 mph/240 kph)

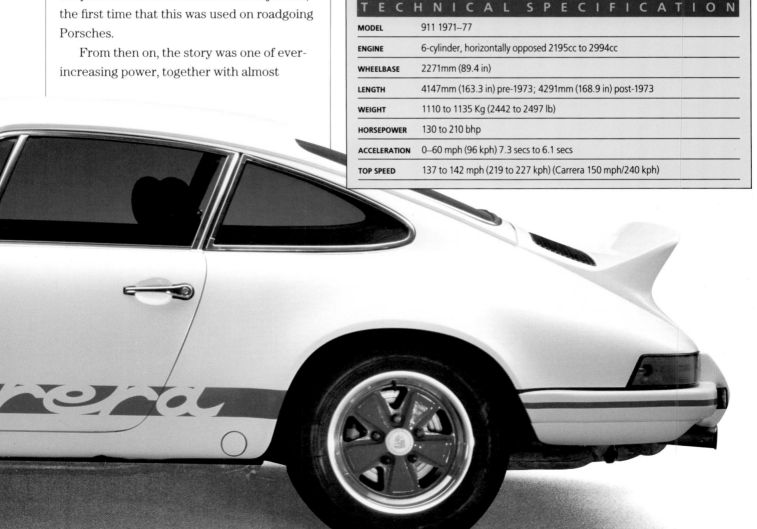

allow all cars to run on 93 octane (research) fuel, equivalent to 'regular' 88 octane by the American R+M/2 system, but power still went up: the 911T surpassed the original 911, with 140 bhp; and the others gained 10 bhp each for 165 bhp on the 911E and 190 bhp on the 911S. The five-speed box was revised, with 1-4 in the 'H' and fifth on the 'dog-leg', and for a brief interval (late 1971 to late 1972), the oil filler for the dry-sump engine was taken to the outside of the car, between the right rear wheel and the door, with a flap over the top like the flap over the fuel filler. This admirable feature was deleted when gas station attendants persisted in trying to fill the oil tank with gasoline.

At the same time – late 1972 – the Carrera name was revived for the 911RS (*rennsport*), a competition car that was just about street-legal, except in the United States where it was

stymied by emission controls and could only be used on the track. All sound insulation was stripped out, as was any unnecessary trim; the rear lid was fibreglass; there were no rear seats; the sheet metal was thinner; and even the windshield was thinner and lighter. As with the 911R, the weight was under 2000 lb (910 kg), but the extra power from the engine was achieved largely through a dramatic increase in bore size, from 84 mm to 90 mm.

This would not have been possible with the old Biral cylinders, which could only be bored to about 87.5 mm, so new 'Nickasil' cylinders were used – light alloy, lined with a nickel/silicon carbide compound. This gave an easy 210 bhp, and the car was so popular that instead of the 500 originally planned, the total production run was about 1600, of which some 600 were actually trimmed and outfitted to 911S specifications.

The 1973 911 Carrera RSR captured three international and seven national championships in its first season. Its career started at the Daytona 24-hour race, beating more powerful cars such as Ferrari, Matra and Mirage-Ford.

This much power had the potential to create serious handling problems in a car so light, so the front air dam was augmented by the first of the 'ducktail' spoilers which are now so familiar on Porsches, and the rear wheels were given 175 mm (7 in) rims for really wide rubber. Even this was not enough for some people, though: the 2806cc 911RSR, with over 300 bhp, won the 1975 Targa Florio – by now a familiar Porsche stamping-ground

for more than half-a-century, ever since the little Sascha had won its class in 1922.

The new 2687cc displacement was standardized on the other models for the 1974 model year, together with fuel injection, but horsepower actually came down in the interests of increased flexibility and ease of driving. The drops were not great – 150 bhp for the regular 911 and 175 bhp for both the 911S and the Carrera – but they were enough to make many people cry into their beer about the passing of a Golden Age. With the benefit of hindsight we can see that this was merely a hysterical reaction to the (largely manufactured) 'oil crisis', but at the time, it looked bad.

Of course, if you could afford to disregard the hysteria, and if you were not burdened with American emission regulations, you could buy another version of the 911, bearing the RS or RSR designations, with an engine bored out to 95 mm to give 2993cc. Of the 109

ABOVE AND INSET
A 1974 Carrera 2.7, uncluttered and fast enough for any normal road use.

LEFT *The RS (left) and its racing version, the RSR (right), both of 1974 vintage. Note the fatter rear arches on the RSR.*

ABOVE *The dash of the 1974/5 Porsche 911.*

LEFT *By 1975 the 911 Targa had a fixed rear window, although the roof was made in a single piece and could still be removed. Most 911s carried the standard American-style bumpers.*

examples made, only 49 were bare racers; the other 60 were road cars, albeit with varying levels of trim and sound insulation. For your money you got 230 bhp in the 'cooking' RS, and 330 bhp in the 'full chat' RSR with the slider throttles (early butterfly-valve models were a mere 315 bhp). At this point, of course, we are looking at eight times the original power output of the 356!

It must have seemed to many, in the mid-1970s, that the 911 was reaching the limits of its development. After all, the major development of the 356 had effectively covered little over a decade: development of the early cars was slow, and for the last couple of years, they were merely coasting. The basic 911 certainly did not see many changes in 1975, though the Carrera went back up to a respectable 210 bhp from the S-level 175 bhp of the previous year; it was to rise and fall with the whims of the American government for some time to come. The major innovation of

TECHNICAL SPECIFICATION			
MODEL	911 SC 1976–83 (zinc coated body)		
ENGINE	2994cc		
WHEELBASE	2271mm (89.4 in)		
LENGTH	4291mm (168.9 in)		
WEIGHT	1160 kg (2552 lb)		
HORSEPOWER	204 bhp		
ACCELERATION	0–60 mph (96 kph) 5.7 secs 0–62 mph (99 kph) 5.4 secs		
TOP SPEED	148 mph (236 kph)		

1976 was the sort of thing one might expect from a 'mature' product: the adoption, at last, of a serious major-league rust-proofing programme (with galvanized-steel sheet metal), because rust was something that had always troubled all roadgoing Porsches, except perhaps in Southern California and the American desert states.

The year 1975 did however see the arrival of the Turbo, with the 2993cc displacement of

ABOVE *The 911 Turbo was announced at the Paris Salon in 1974 and production started in 1975. This is a 1976 three-litre model.*

the old RS and RSR, but with an altogether staggering increase in horsepower to 260 bhp at 5500 rpm, almost a quarter as much again as the Carrera: 'scalded cat' acceleration was there for the asking. Then, for the 1978 model year, there was even more of the same: no Carrera (though the 911SC was up to 180 bhp with a taller, flatter torque curve), but an even more mind-boggling 300 bhp at 5500 rpm on the standard, roadgoing Turbo, now bored to 97 mm and stroked to 74.4 mm for a capacity of 3299cc.

The 0-60 times of the last of the economy-sized Volkswagen Beetles, were in the 15–20 second range. In the same time, the 3.3 Turbo could hit 120 mph; *Motor* magazine got 19.1 seconds. A hundred miles an hour came up in 12.3 seconds – a very respectable 0-60 time for most family cars – and the 0-60 time was a mere 5.3 seconds. 'Muscle' cars may have been past their peak, but if they were, no-one in Zuffenhausen had noticed. The top speed of the Turbo was well in excess of 2.5 miles (4 km) a minute.

LEFT *The Porsche 911 turbo, introduced in 1983.*

TECHNICAL SPECIFICATION	
MODEL	911 Turbo/SE 1976–89 (New model due 1990/1)
ENGINE	6-cylinder, horizontally opposed 2994cc to 3299cc
WHEELBASE	2271mm (89.4 in)
LENGTH	4290mm (168.9 in)
WEIGHT	1142 to 1303 kg (2513 to 2866 lb)
HORSEPOWER	260 to 330 bhp
ACCELERATION	0–60 mph (96 kph) 6 secs to 0–62 mph (99 kph) 5.4 secs
TOP SPEED	155 to 171 mph (248 to 273 kph)

Driving at these speeds – beyond 2 miles a minute, say – is an extraordinary experience, and one which fewer and fewer people have had the chance to enjoy. The first few times you do it, you are struck by two things. One is that roads which you had always thought were fairly straight are suddenly revealed as being considerably more twisted than you remembered. The other is that it is almost as if you are standing still, and the rest of the world is rushing past you very, very quickly. If there are any other cars on the road, you had better

hope that the drivers are awake: you may well pass them at speed differentials of 30 – 50 miles (48 – 80 km) an hour. As you exceed 140 mph (224 kph) your concentration becomes so tight that you are aware of nothing but the road, the car, and (dimly) the whine of the engine.

This is one of the reasons why fast driving really is much more dangerous in the United States than in Europe. The complete lack of lane discipline in the United States, with passing permitted on both sides, combines

LEFT AND TOP RIGHT *The three-litre Turbo engine was uprated to 3.3L and could now accelerate to 100km/h in just 5.4 seconds, with a top speed of 260km/h. This is the 1980 911 3.3 Turbo.*

with the tendency of many American drivers to treat their cars as extensions of their drawing rooms, where they can listen to music or engage in conversation and only incidentally point the car in the general direction in which they intend to go. Fast drivers in, say, Germany can usually rely on the other fellow being awake; fast drivers in the United States can make no such assumptions – and besides, if they catch you at more than 100 mph (160 kph), they are after locking you up, because they *know* that no-one could possibly control a car at that speed. An enduring fantasy, when you are driving at high speed on the 101, is imagining the look on a CHP speed-cop's face if only he could see a German autobahn . . .

LEFT *The 1980 Porsche 911 3.3-litre turbo.*

In the early-to-mid 1980s, the United States really became the poor relation when it came to Porsche sales. In 1979, for the first time, more Porsches had been sold in their native Germany than in the United States, and American emission and safety controls meant that the really exotic vehicles could no longer even be considered for US homologation. Uniformly less powerful than their European counterparts (which seemed pretty much to be on a plateau anyway), Porsches shifted from being *fast* cars to being *luxury* cars. A true convertible finally appeared in 1982, supplementing the Targa style, and (as usual) Porsche continued to offer all their engines in all their body styles. Many an adolescent fantasy centred around a Porsche 911 Turbo convertible.

Back in Europe, Porsche were keeping the faith by introducing the four-wheel-drive 959

derivative of the 911, though the visual resemblance between the 959 and the 911 was clearer than the actual mechanical relationship; under the skin, the car owed more to the 935 racer. The 959 used a Kevlar composite body, hollow magnesium wheels, electronically controlled full-time four wheel drive with continuously variable traction splitting front to rear (with manual override) and a twin-turbo version of the 935 flat 6 (itself a 911 derivative, as described in Chapter 8). With a minimum of 400 bhp, depending on whether you wanted the basic 190 mph road car or a proper, fast sports-racer, feeding through a six-speed gearbox, the base price was well over £100,000 (about $200,000). Porsche did not even try to 'Americanize' the car; it was just impossible. As they had done before, they offered a cosmetic and (slightly) aerodynamic package which gave the American 911s a 935/959 look, but it was an expensive way to get not very much more in return.

Then, for the 1989 model year, they set the automotive world on its ear by producing three new 911s – and, better still, by making them available to the suffering Americans. The 911 Speedster was a homage to the old

ABOVE *A 1981 911SC 3-litre coupe.*

RIGHT *A 911 SC 3.0L Targa being put through its paces on the German autobahn, 1982.*

LEFT *The powerhouse of the 959: 0-60 in just 3.7 seconds, and a top speed that exceeds 190mph.*

OVERLEAF *The brand new Speedster for 1990-91.*

'bathtub', essentially a fair-weather car (though much better outfitted than its 356 predecessor), and only 800 were made. The Club Sport was a lightened 911 Carrera coupé, minus such details as air conditioning, arm rests, electric windows, power door locks, door armrests and rear seats, for a saving of 155 lb (70 kg); and the surprise was the 911 Carrera 4.

This was a true four-wheel-drive 911, introduced in coupé form with a 247 bhp version of the 3.6 litre flat 6. The floor pan was, however, the first completely rethought 'chassis' since the introduction of the 901, with MacPherson struts on the front and semi-trailing rear suspension. Electronically controlled locking differentials controlled the power to the wheels, an anti-lock braking system (ABS) was standard, and purists decried the disappearing spoiler on the back, which raised automatically at about 40 mph and lowered automatically at about 6 mph.

In 1990, the Carrera 2 appellation was applied, not illogically, to a two-wheel-drive version of the Carrera 4, and both 2WD and 4WD were available (once again) on all three of the 'standard' body styles, Coupe, Targa and Cabriolet.

The Carrera 2 also introduced a 'Tiptronic' automatic gearbox, with a two-slot H-gate; on the left, it is a conventional 4-speed automatic, while on the right it is very similar to a motorcycle gearbox; a smart pull backwards changes down by one gear from whatever gear you happen to be in, and a smart flick forwards will change up one gear.

RIGHT The ultimate road car? Possibly the ultimate Porsche ... This is the 959.

BELOW The 1990 911s are far more rounded, although the classic 911 lines were kept.

At the time of writing the newest Porsche was the 911 Turbo Coupé, using the new floor-pan from the Carrera 4/Carrera 2 and the 3.3 litre displacement engine, turbocharged, twin-plugged, and delivering a blinding 315 bhp – legitimately described by Porsche as 'the quickest 911 ever' with a 0-60 time of 4.8 seconds and a top speed of 168 mph (268 kph). Staying at the forefront of 1990s supercars was not a bad trick for a model that had recently celebrated its 25th birthday, and which Porsche themselves were not sure could survive the 1970s. Admittedly, it boasted a new chassis, new rear suspension

BELOW *The 911 Carrera 2.*

with automatic toe correction, new wheels (17 in (425 mm) diameter, 7 in (175 mm) wide at the front and 9 in (225 mm) wide at the rear): all these features are a logical progression in the 'faking out' of the inherent vices of rear-engined cars, and they now push the performance envelope so far out that for most Porsche drivers, any questions of handling limitations are irrelevant. They have also come a long way from the days when they used to bolt weights inside the ends of the front bumpers . . .

I had to stop writing this book just before the 1990 Frankfurt Motor Show: the

TECHNICAL SPECIFICATION	
MODEL	911 Carrera 2/4 1983 to date
ENGINE	6-cylinder, horizontally opposed 3164cc to 3600cc
WHEELBASE	2272mm (89.4 in)
LENGTH	4250mm (167.3 in)
WEIGHT	1350 kg (2970 lb) to 1450 kg (3319 lb)
HORSEPOWER	231 to 250 bhp
ACCELERATION	0–62 mph (99 kph) 6.1 secs to 5.7 secs
TOP SPEED	152 to 161 mph (243 to 257 kph)

ABOVE *A 911 Carrera 2/4.*

TOP RIGHT *A 1991 911 Turbo.*

RIGHT *The dashboard of the 911 Carrera 2 cabriolet. The hood opens and closes at the touch of a button.*

LEFT *The engine, a six-cylinder 3.6L, is the most powerful of the range, producing 250bhp.*

publishers just would not let me have any more time, even though I told them (like a gold miner expecting the Big Strike any minute) that the 911 Turbo Carrera was inevitable, and that we should wait for that. They were right, of course; let any Porsche enthusiast have his way, and the book would never be finished. It is a very safe bet, though, to say that the 911 is still a very long way from finished. Indeed, it completely outlived one potential 'replacement' model, the mid-engined 914 and 914/6, which are the subject of the next chapter.

MID-ENGINE 5

Just about all of Porsche's pure racing designs (as distinct from sports/racing cars) placed the engine between the rear wheels and the driver. The advantages are numerous: compactness, a short, light, efficient drive train, excellent balance and low polar moments of inertia. The last means that a mid-engined car will continue to go unprotestingly around corners at speeds which would be asking for breakaway in a front- or rear-engined car. When it finally lets go, though, you will be travelling very quickly indeed and you will be in serious trouble unless you have the skills of Caracciola or Rosenberg.

The disadvantages of putting the engine in the middle of a road car are however almost as numerous as the advantages of putting the engine in the middle of a racing car. Passenger space and luggage space are both reduced; sound insulation is more difficult, the cockpit may well get very hot, and engine access is limited. In racing, you can pretty much ignore all this inconvenience. However in building road cars, you need to judge your audience carefully, which is why there have only been a handful of mid-engined sports cars, even fewer of which have been commercially successful, mostly at the most expensive end of the market: Ferrari, Lamborghini. Remember the Lotus Europa, the Fiat X1/9, the Pontiac Fiero – many countries have tried them – and the Porsche 914.

In fact, the Porsche 914 was a Porsche only in the United States; elsewhere it was sold as a Volkswagen-Porsche and it was generally referred to as a VolksPorsche. To a few, who

RIGHT *Introduced in 1969, the mid-engined 914 sports car was a joint venture with Volkswagen. This is a Type 914/4, which used a VW engine of 1679cc.*

were unaware of the connotations of the word, it was a VoPo, which is also the abbreviation for the *Volks Polizei* or East German border guards who enjoyed a reputation roughly equivalent to the S.S.

On paper it looked good. Two engines were offered; a 1679cc flat-4 Volkswagen pushrod engine with 80 bhp on tap, and a 1991cc flat-6 Porsche engine with an overhead cam on each bank and 110 bhp; a very similar

engine, in fact, to a 911T. It was well-balanced, with 46/54 front/rear distribution, so it cornered *better* than a 911. It was light, it was quick, it was modestly priced, at around half as much as a 911; it seemed to have everything going for it.

Unfortunately, it laboured under two major disadvantages. One was that it was unbelievably ugly, especially with the Targa top removed, when it looked as if it was going

RIGHT *The Porsche badge on a 1990 928GT.*

CENTER AND BELOW
Following the 914/4 came the 914/6, which used the engine of the 1969 911T, and the 916, which never saw production. Pictured here is the 916 of 1970.

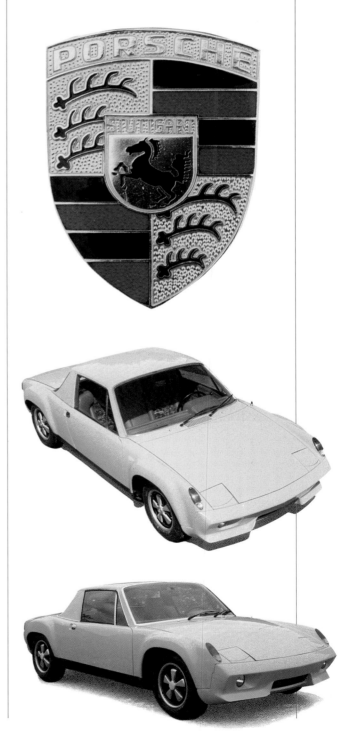

to break in half. The other was that it had
PORSCHE written on it, and that people
therefore expected more than they got. It also
had some other drawbacks which, although
not as great as those two, were still pretty
convincing. It was extremely noisy; the gear
changing linkages were infuriatingly
imprecise, despite the use of a 911 gearbox in
both models; the luggage space was barely
adequate, despite having a small trunk at each
end; the cockpit was cramped, with the backs
of the seats hard against the bulkhead; and if
you drove the 914/4 too fast or too far, it
would refuse to restart until it had cooled
down to what it considered a reasonable
working temperature. This last fault was
almost impossible to trace, and may have
involved any or all of the following: fuel
vapour lock (an admitted problem), the
starter, the starter solenoid, or almost
anything else electrical.

The ugliness is something people could
have learned to live with if the car had been as
good as everyone previously hoped. So were
the noise and the lack of luggage space. The
passenger space you could (just about) get
used to. The hot-starting problems could have
been solved with development. But the big,
big problem was that because of the name
PORSCHE everyone expected something very
much better than this. If it had been a car from
an unknown manufacturer, or even a car from
a manufacturer who was branching out into
sports cars for the first time, it would have
enjoyed a considerably more enthusiastic
reception. Nevertheless it was a Porsche that
did not live up to being a Porsche, and no-one
forgave it.

To a certain extent, it was born under a
bad sign. Ferry Porsche and Heinz Nordhoff
conceived it as a car designed by Porsche for
Volkswagen, with Volkswagen retaining the
option to buy back some body shells to fit
their own engines. It would replace
Volkswagen's Karmann Ghia, which was
fading fast, and it would provide Porsche with
a cheap body to modify as they wished. The
body, designed by Gugelot GmbH, had

TECHNICAL SPECIFICATION	
MODEL	914 4/6 916 1970–75
ENGINE	4- or 6-cylinder, horizontally opposed; 1679cc to 1971cc pushrod 4, 1991cc sohc 6
WHEELBASE	2450mm (96.5 in)
LENGTH	3985mm (156.9 in)
WEIGHT	940 to 995 Kg (2068 to 2189 lb)
HORSEPOWER	80 to 110 bhp
ACCELERATION	0–60 mph (96 kph) 12 secs to 8.5 secs
TOP SPEED	108 to 126 mph (172 to 201 kph)

*Three 914/6s entered the
Marathon de la Route
84-hour race at the
Nürburgring in 1970.
The cars were prepared
by the factory and
classed as 'civil' rally
versions', producing
160bhp.*

originally been intended for a front engine, but Butzi and his crew re-worked it until it was functionally very good, though it was a shame they did nothing about the looks.

Then Heinz Nordhoff fell ill and shortly died, and the new head of Volkswagen (Kurt Lotz) turned out to be a bean-counter who wanted more money out of Porsche for each body; much more money. In doing so, he killed the Porsche. From Volkswagen's point of view it was far from a failure – over 127,000 914/4s were made – but it was never the car that everyone had hoped. Because of this, Porsche (who had more to lose by having their name associated with an 'also-ran') discontinued the 914/6 in 1972, and only a handful (probably fewer than 50) were made in that year, so they are very sought-after motor cars. There were only ever 3,360 914/6s in total.

With the demise of the 914/6, though, Volkswagen installed a significantly more

BELOW Ferry Porsche received a 914/8 from the company for his 60th birthday. Only two were made, the other being used for test purposes by Porsche's chief designer at the time, Ferdinand Piech.

powerful engine in the same body, a 1971cc flat 4 delivering 95 bhp. This 1973 914/4 is a considerably more desirable car than the earlier models, because it also has the much improved side-shifter transaxle, and an adjustable driver's seat.

A remarkable number of these cars seem to have survived in Southern California. They were not, however, greatly sought after: in the late 1980s the 914/4 was little above 'banger' status, and could be picked up for a song.

There was, however, a brief postscript to the 914 story. After some success with a competition version of the 914/6 (the 914/6GT, which won the GT class at Le Mans in 1970 and finished first, second and third in the Marathon de la Route in the same year), Porsche seriously considered a redesigned version of their own, to be called the 916.

It was immensely better looking than the 914, with an integrated self-coloured bumper,

ABOVE AND LEFT *One of the two 914/8s produced. These cars used the eight-cylinder race engine fitted to the 908 sports car.*

front spoilers, dramatically flared rectangular arches over very much more attractive (and wider) wheels, virtually no chrome, and the 155 bhp 2.4 litre fuel-injected engine from the 911E. With only 2200 lb (1000 kg) or so to propel, the engine gave truly spectacular performance, and (as usual with Porsche) there was room for plenty of development, including even the Carrera and Turbo engines. About 20 916s were built, and brochures were printed for a launch at the Paris Motor Show in 1971; and then suddenly, the marketing department got cold feet and called the whole project off. The cars went to members of the Porsche family and to a few special customers.

An even more dramatic case of 'what might have been' is afforded by the two 914s which were fitted with the flat-8, 3-litre racing engine, one of which went to Ferry Porsche on his 60th birthday and the other of which went to Ferdinand Piëch. These were hardly feasible as production cars, but they are certainly evidence that at Porsche they believe in mid-engined road cars!

HERESY AND REFORMATION

A s far back as the 1960s Porsche had begun to wonder about the future of the 911, and indeed about the future of the whole rear-engined concept which was principally a result of its Volkswagen ancestry. They were always worried that one day – or at least, one year – the demand for the 911 would fall dramatically, and that they would be caught flat-footed without a replacement. The mid-engined 914/6 or even 916 might or might not have done the trick; when it became apparent that it wouldn't, Porsche management started casting around for an alternative.

BELOW *Porsche introduced the 924 in 1976. It used many components produced by VW, and was the first Porsche to use a front-mounted water-cooled engine.*

Although Porsche had had their fingers burnt with Volkswagen before, they not unnaturally looked to their old friends, who were going through a bad time as it became obvious that they could not go on selling the

T E C H N I C A L	S P E C I F I C A T I O N
MODEL	924 1976–89
ENGINE	4-cylinder in-line 1984cc to 2497cc
WHEELBASE	2400mm (94.5 in)
LENGTH	4213mm (165.9 in)
WEIGHT	1080 Kg (2376 lb)
HORSEPOWER	125 (European model) to 150
ACCELERATION	0–62 mph (99 kph) 9.6 secs to 8.5 secs
TOP SPEED	125 to 130 mph (200 to 208 kph) (Carrera 150 mph/240 kph)

T E C H N I C A L	S P E C I F I C A T I O N
MODEL	924 Turbo 1978–82
ENGINE	4-cylinder in line 1984cc
WHEELBASE	2400mm (94.5 in)
LENGTH	4213mm (165.9 in)
WEIGHT	1182 kg (2601 lb)
HORSEPOWER	170 to 245 bhp
ACCELERATION	0–62 mph (99 kph) 7.8 secs to 6.9 secs
TOP SPEED	132 to 150 mph (211 to 240 kph)

outdated Beetle forever. Kurt Lotz had by this time left Volkswagen, after a very brief tenure, and Rudolf Leiding came in. Porsche had been working on a prototype for Volkswagen with a water-cooled four lying on its side under the rear seat, the EA 266: an excellent idea for an ultra-compact power train in a mid-engined car, and one which Porsche also had hopes of as the basis for a future car of their own. Leiding, though, wanted to join the rush to front-wheel drive, which led to the VW Passat and VW Polo (which had been developed at Audis) and in due course to the Golf.

He also wanted a flagship, though, so he asked Porsche to develop such a vehicle, which was coded EA 425 at Volkswagen. Then, in 1974, Leiding was given the push as being too visionary and not concerned enough with bean-counting, and Toni Schmücker took over just as EA 425 – otherwise known as Porsche Type 924 – was nearing completion. He in his turn knocked the project on the

head, partly as a genuine economy and partly as a reaction against introducing a new sports car in the middle of a so-called 'oil-crisis'.

By a complex series of 'everybody-wins' deals, Porsche got to keep the Type 924. This used a number of VW-Audi parts, and kept open the NSU plant at Neckarsulm which Schmücker had been planning to close as a part of his economy drive. The only problem was that Porsche didn't want a front-wheel drive car. They also had the V8-engined 928 in mind, and they needed a body shell (and a drive layout) that could handle both engines.

ABOVE *The 924 was aimed at those who could not stretch to the 911. Good mileage and better-than-normal service intervals helped to keep the running costs down.*

What they did, therefore, was to put the transmission at the back, in a transaxle, which gave an excellently balanced car with 48 per cent of the weight at the front and 52 per cent at the rear. It also looked good in the marketing literature.

This layout made for an interesting compromise. A really skilled driver will almost certainly be able to throw a 911 around more than he could a 924; but because of the weight layout and the polar moments of inertia, the 924 gives much more warning of when it is going to slide, and the initial slide is very much more controllable. You still need to be something more than a novice to control any sort of car when it starts to go, and if opposite lock and steering with the accelerator are foreign concepts to you, a 924 will bite you just as surely as any other car (including a 914) when if finally does let go; but you need to be very unlucky, very stupid, or very skilled ever to take any modern Porsche outside its 'performance envelope'.

The other remarkable thing about the Porsche 924 was the extent to which it was a 'bitza' (bitza Audi, bitza Volkswagen, bitza Porsche . . .)

The 86.5 × 84.4 mm Heron-head four had a swept volume of 1984cc, with a single overhead cam. An Audi design, it also appeared in the Audi 100, a VW van, and rather improbably the AMC Gremlin. It gave a respectable 125 bhp at 5800 rpm, until it was got at for the American market, when it dropped to a barely acceptable 100 bhp at 5500 rpm.

The transaxle was another Audi part, with four speeds and a non-Porsche synchromesh. The front suspension, curiously enough, was a Volkswagen Beetle MacPherson strut with lower wishbones from the Rabbit /Golf/ Scirroco; the trailing arms at the back came from the Super Beetle; steering was from the Rabbit; brakes were Beetle drums at the rear, Audi discs at the front. The body was attractive without being distinctively Porsche, despite the conscious decision to hide the air intakes under the high front bumper and create a certain visual continuity with the rear-engined cars which, of course, had never had grilles. It was designed by the studio of Tony Lapine. The car entered production in November 1975.

Initially, the 924 suffered at the hands of the critics in much the same way that the 914 had done. It was very much prettier, to be sure, but is also had PORSCHE written on it, and expectations were therefore very high; one might fairly say, unrealistically high. In particular, the ride was criticized as being harsh, with far too much transmission of road noise through the wheels and bodywork; a solid *thump-thump-thump* seemed to echo through the whole car as you traversed the expansion joints on a bridge, or if you had the misfortune to be riding on an American

BELOW *The 1981 924 Turbo engine was first introduced to the public in 1979. It used a KKK blower and could push the car from 0-60 in under 7 seconds. Shown to the public at the 1977 Geneva Motor Salon, the 928 used a front-mounted V8 engine of 4474cc.*

concrete freeway such as the 101 between Santa Barbara and Goleta. Wind noise worried some people – though they were mostly the type who drive with the windows closed and the air-conditioner on – and there was no doubt that if you were too free with the loud pedal, the engine could add its note to the general cacophony, but not in an enjoyable way; it was a throbby, complaining sort of noise which made you want to ease off.

If you could stand the noise, though, the 125 mph (200 kph) top speed was not too shabby; the 0-60 time of 8.2 seconds was definitely on the respectable side of ordinary; and the fuel consumption, at 25 miles to the Imperial gallon (20 miles to the US gallon) was entirely praiseworthy.

As is usual with Porsche the answers to the criticisms were evolutionary rather than revolutionary. A three-speed automatic was made optional almost immediately, for those who wanted to drive a Porsche simply because it was the thing to do, rather than because it was a car they wanted to enjoy driving. In 1977 the transmission was replaced

There matters rested for a while because in 1977, at the March Geneva Salon, Porsche had unveiled a similar looking car which was powered by an altogether more impressive motor, the 4.5 litre V8.

The new car was called a 928, and it is impossible not to suspect that Porsche 'bent' their own type-number rules to make the 924 a 4-cylinder and the 928 an 8-cylinder.

T E C H N I C A L S P E C I F I C A T I O N	
MODEL	928 1977 to date
ENGINE	V-8 4474cc, enlarged steadily to 4957cc
WHEELBASE	2500mm (98.4 in)
LENGTH	4445mm (175 in)
WEIGHT	Over 1450 Kg (3190 lb)
HORSEPOWER	240 bhp to 330 bhp, with development
ACCELERATION	0–60 mph (96 kph) 7 secs to 0–62 mph (99 kph) 5.4 secs
TOP SPEED	140 to 170 mph (224 to 272 kph)

LEFT *The interior of the 928 was spacious and well-equipped as this 1984 model shows.*

BELOW *A Porsche 928S.*

with a five-speed in the 'Getrag' layout with first gear in the dog-leg and second to fifth in the 'H'. In 1979 this was replaced again, with another Audi-derived gearbox which had 1-4 in the 'H' and fifth in the dog-leg.

More to the point, 1979 also saw a turbocharged version with a new cylinder head and more torque (at 181 instead of 143 lb ft at 3500 rpm) as well as a lot more power; 170 bhp instead of 125 bhp. For the American market, the increase was limited only to 150 bhp, but even this was still very welcome.

The choice of a V8 is at first glance curious. Admittedly, it is a 90° V8, probably the best possible layout, and it seems unlikely that there was room for a flat-8 even if they had wanted one. Certainly, a V8 can be made smooth; but so can a straight 6, as evidenced by Jaguar, and the idea of a V12 must surely have crossed the minds of the gentlemen in Zuffenhausen. But a V8 is compact, so it would fit into a relatively short, shallow engine bay with a sloping hood and it can certainly be made to give very adequate power outputs.

European models and a barely reduced 230 bhp at 5250 rpm for the American version.

Unlike the 924, though, the transmission was in front of the differential, and instead of being all-indirect, fifth was straight through. This made for a quieter box, especially at cruising speeds.

Again unlike the 924 the suspension was not a parts-bin 'bitza'; there were unequal-length wishbones, derived from racing practice, at the front, and a totally new Porsche design which they called the

BELOW *This is a 928 S Coupe.*

The actual capacity was 4474cc, achieved with a 90 mm bore and 78.9 mm stroke, with a linerless alloy block and alloy heads, each with its own single overhead cam driven by a toothed belt – another feature to drive the traditionalists mad, because chains or (better still) extremely complicated spur and bevel drives were long considered *de rigeur* in Porsche engine designs. The belt is quieter, simpler, cheaper, and requires less maintenance (though it should be changed at the recommended intervals), but to a Porsche addict, you are not talking about engineering; you are talking about fundamental beliefs about Life, the Universe and Everything.

Like the 924, the 928 was fuel-injected, and at the time of its introduction the power output was a respectable, though by no means excessive, 240 bhp at 5500 rpm for the

'Weissach axle' at the back. Both front and rear suspension designs owed a lot to the lessons that Porsche had learned in racing.

To 'add lightness,' the doors, hood and even front fenders were of light alloy, and plastic was used wherever it was suitable – for example, to cover the energy-absorbing bumpers and make them blend smoothly with the body.

There were, however, a number of weighty gewgaws which must easily have offset this saving, such as power windows, central pneumatically-actuated (!) locking, air-conditioning (including a cooled glove compartment, a valuable feature for photographers who did not want to cook their film), electrically adjusted and heated outside mirrors, and more.

In short, it was a most improbable vehicle; a light, fast luxury car. This is by no means an

The 1990 928 GT uses the powerful 5 litre V8 32 valve engine, capable of a top speed in excess of 170 mph. The driver has space and comfort with modified suspension, wider wheels, and tyres to increase road holding abilities.

unknown breed – Bristol Cars have been doing it sublimely well since the late 1940s – but it is certainly a most unusual breed.

It was also a giant, at least by Porsche standards, with a dry weight of more than 3000 lb (1363 kg), though in 1980 they managed to lose about 220 lb (100 kg) of that by a number of expedients which in no way compromised either the performance or the luxury of the car, such as making the torque tube between the engine and the transmission out of light alloy.

Before they went through the weight reduction programme, though, they went through a power enhancement programme in 1979. A 2mm increase in bore gave 4664cc, and together with improved breathing, dual exhausts and a compression ratio which rose from 9:1 to 10:1 this resulted in a full 300 bhp, with an attendant top speed of 155 mph (248 kph) and a 0–100 mph time of less than 15 seconds; it was rightly named the 928S.

Some attention to the aerodynamics also got the drag coefficient (C_d) below 0.40 to about 0.38; nothing to write home about, but a worthwhile improvement, and markedly better than the old figure which was embarrassingly similar to some very ordinary and unpretentious sedans.

Once again, the unfortunate Americans found out what it means to live in a free country; they weren't allowed to buy it. Not until 1983 did they get an 'S' version and even then, power was rated a very modest 234 bhp. Of course, in the meantime they had (as usual) been offered a sop in the form of a 928S look-a-like with go-faster cosmetics and even a limited-slip differential, but they still had to get by with 231 bhp (it had gone up by 1 bhp in 1980).

The real fun came in 1985, though, when the V8 grew an extra camshaft on each bank of cylinders to become a genuine double-knocker. To give the extra cams something to do, the engine was bored another 3mm to a nice, round 100mm for a total swept volume of

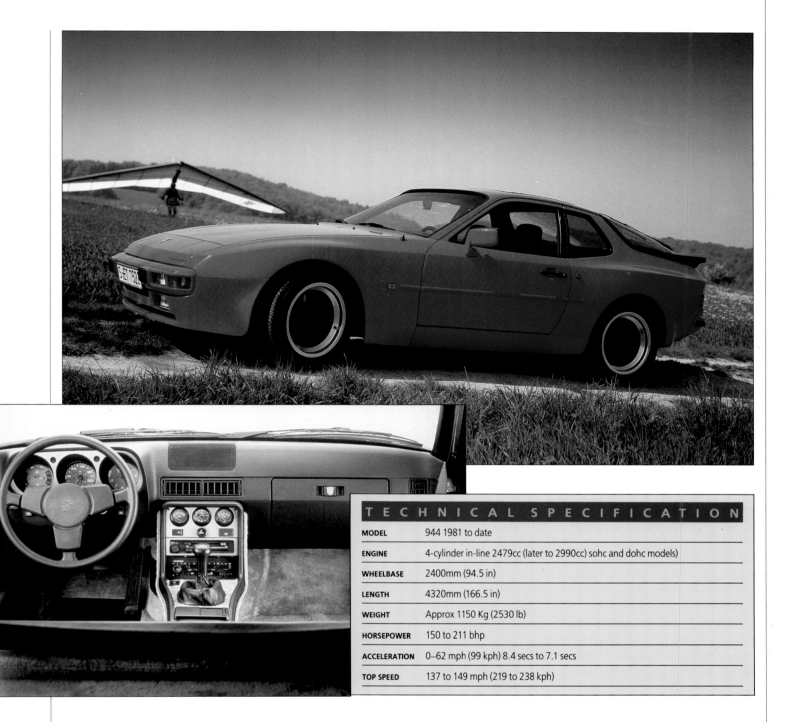

MODEL	944 1981 to date
ENGINE	4-cylinder in-line 2479cc (later to 2990cc) sohc and dohc models)
WHEELBASE	2400mm (94.5 in)
LENGTH	4320mm (166.5 in)
WEIGHT	Approx 1150 Kg (2530 lb)
HORSEPOWER	150 to 211 bhp
ACCELERATION	0–62 mph (99 kph) 8.4 secs to 7.1 secs
TOP SPEED	137 to 149 mph (219 to 238 kph)

4957cc. Even for the United States, a good 300 bhp was on tap, and this was boosted in subsequent model years until, at the time of writing, it was not far short of 350 bhp. Electronic knock sensors, which adjusted timing automatically, allowed the engine to run on unleaded fuel of almost any octane rating, and a 1987 redesign of the nose and front spoiler, together with a stand-off rear spoiler, finally got the C_d down to a very fair 0.35 with virtually no lift at high speed and a top speed of over 160 mph (256 kph) even

TOP With flared arches, wider wheels and a new engine, the 944 was an altogether superior car than the 924.

ABOVE Here is the 1984 version and above is its well equipped dashboard and controls.

with the automatic transmission (162 mph [260 kph] automatic, 165 mph [268 kph] manual – a fairly inconsequential distinction at those velocities).

Although it had not been done on a production car at the time of writing, at least one works car had been turbocharged. We can only guess at the results, but 400 bhp should have been so easy as to excite no comment; in fact, 500 bhp should be possible. And, of course, there is room in the existing block for at least another half litre of displacement.

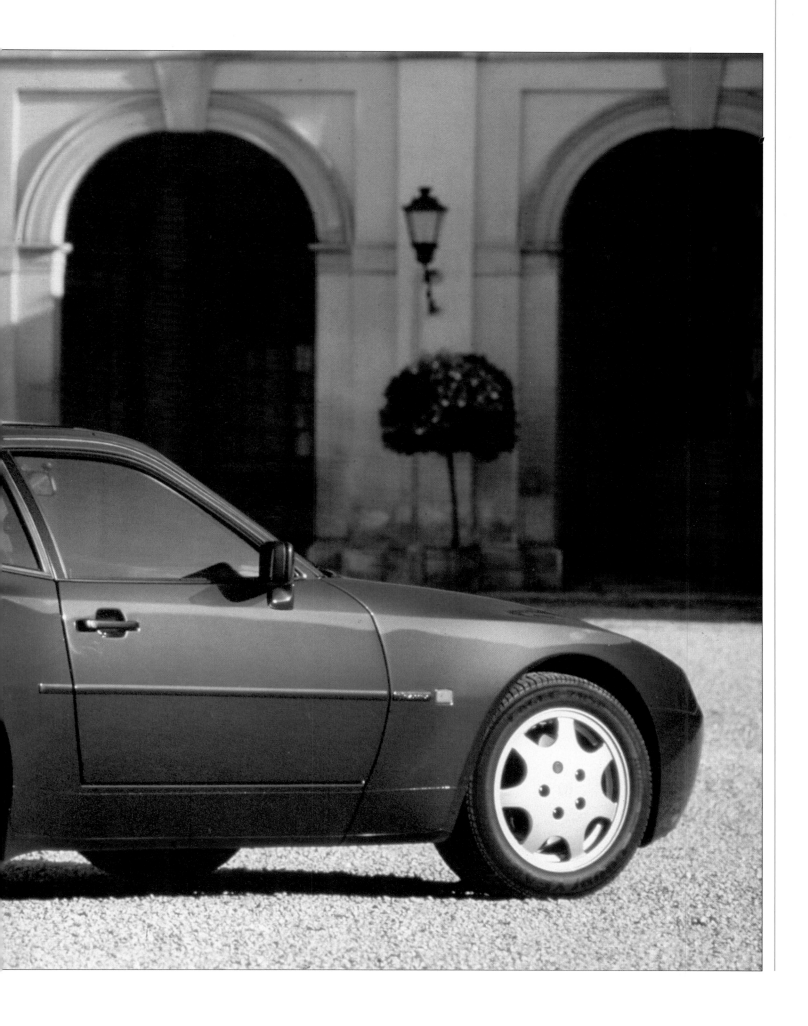

Meanwhile, back at the ranch, the original 924 languished somewhat unloved; but Porsche had plans for changing all that too, with the 944.

As we have seen, the 924 engine was a VW/Audi. As we also know, Porsche engineers are constitutionally capable of refraining from improvements to Volkswagen parts; and with the 924 engine, the improvements in question consisted of designing a completely new engine. It was another sohc four, but the resemblances pretty much stopped there.

It owed a good deal to the engine in the 928, though to call it 'half a 928' is wide of the

mark; not a single major component is interchangeable with the V8. It was significantly bigger than the 924 engine, at 100mm × 78.9mm for a swept volume of 2479 cc, and (as with the V8), the Americans only got a little less peak power than the Europeans: 150 bhp at 5500 rpm instead of 160 bhp at 5800 rpm. The American version had a much lower compression ratio, though, at 9.5:1 instead of 10.6:1.

The problem with a big, powerful in-line four is, however, that it can be distinctly 'lumpy'; *aficionados* of such things as early Triumph TRs and the 4-cylinder Big Healys

BELOW *The 1990 944 turbo, a direct decendant of the racers that have been competing in the 944 Turbo cup races.*

will know all about this. The solution to this problem was demonstrated by Fred Lanchester as early as 1911, with twin contra-rotating balance shafts, but the technology had been developed by several other companies and by the late 1970s Mitsubishi held the patents on the best version. After looking to see if they could improve on the Japanese system, Porsche engineers decided that it would be a lot more cost-effective to pay Mitsubishi a modest royalty and take it from there. Drive was by toothed belt, which disgraced itself on its first outing (with the engine concealed in a much-modified 924) at Le Mans in 1981, where one of the balance shafts slipped a tooth and instead of reducing roughness, added to it. Even at that, the car finished third in its class and seventh overall.

This solved the objections about the lack of power, and forestalled possible objections to a rough-running engine. Now, what about the general lack of smoothness?

The expedient taken to solve this was extraordinary, involving rubber engine mounts filled with antifreeze; but in the middle of the mount was a divider or septum with a small hole in it, which allowed the antifreeze to flow to and fro, thereby acting very much like a tiny shock absorber. More conventional rubber mounts were used at the back to control the transaxle, and to top it all off, the steering rack was also mounted to the chassis by rubber mountings.

The result was a spectacular reduction in vibration, as Norton had demonstrated many years before with their 'isolastic' engine mountings; but it also meant that engine mountings, more than ever before, were an item to be inspected regularly and replaced when necessary, though 'when necessary' would not be often and would be extremely unlikely to affect the first owner of the vehicle.

The body of the 924 was somewhat modified, with flared wheel-arches, a front air dam, and a small rear spoiler; the suspension was improved slightly, but significantly; and the finished car was turned loose in 1982.

Its reception, except among the most pusillanimous of 911 addicts, was ecstatic. Not only was it all that the 924 should have been,

ABOVE *Comprehensive and without unnecessary distractions, the 944 dashboard has been designed for driver comfort and easy use.*

and wasn't; it was also a 'real' Porsche despite the fact that the engine was in the wrong place and cooled by the wrong fluid. It was 'real' because it went like a Porsche should go (which the 924 didn't) and because it was still a car to which many people could aspire, unlike the 928 with its stratospheric price tag. Admittedly, the price rose very rapidly – in the important American market, from $18,450 at introduction to $25,500 only three years later – but it still remained credible.

Inevitably, they turbocharged it. That was in 1985. The compression ratio was lowered to 8:1, and power went up by about 50 per cent while torque rose by almost 70 per cent, albeit with peak torque at 3500 rpm instead of 3000

rpm. Speed rose from the 120s to the 150s, and the already adequate 0–60 time dropped from around eight seconds to the six-second mark.

A year later, the 944S appeared; again almost inevitably, it was a double-knocker design with 16 valves, and the bottom line was 188 bhp, for a top speed in the 140s (224 kph) (easily!).

So there were now three 944 models.

The next step was also 100 per cent predictable: a 944 Turbo S. The power was now 247 SAE bhp, perhaps 260 DIN, which gave a top speed of better than 160 mph (256 kph) and a 0–60 time of five and a half seconds.

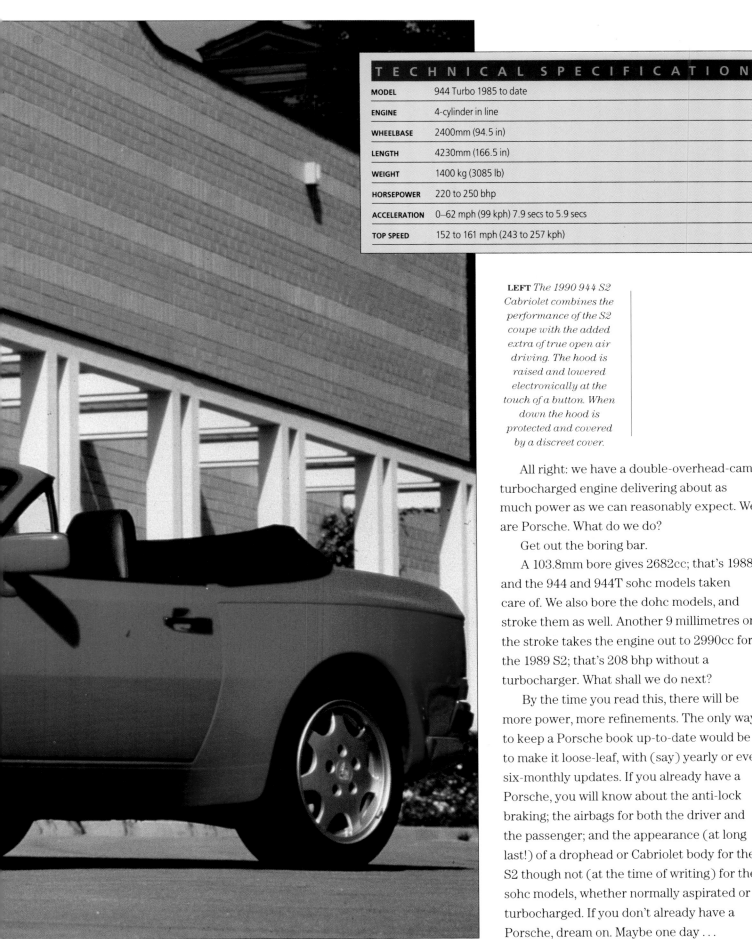

TECHNICAL SPECIFICATION

MODEL	944 Turbo 1985 to date
ENGINE	4-cylinder in line
WHEELBASE	2400mm (94.5 in)
LENGTH	4230mm (166.5 in)
WEIGHT	1400 kg (3085 lb)
HORSEPOWER	220 to 250 bhp
ACCELERATION	0–62 mph (99 kph) 7.9 secs to 5.9 secs
TOP SPEED	152 to 161 mph (243 to 257 kph)

LEFT *The 1990 944 S2 Cabriolet combines the performance of the S2 coupe with the added extra of true open air driving. The hood is raised and lowered electronically at the touch of a button. When down the hood is protected and covered by a discreet cover.*

All right: we have a double-overhead-cam turbocharged engine delivering about as much power as we can reasonably expect. We are Porsche. What do we do?

Get out the boring bar.

A 103.8mm bore gives 2682cc; that's 1988, and the 944 and 944T sohc models taken care of. We also bore the dohc models, and stroke them as well. Another 9 millimetres on the stroke takes the engine out to 2990cc for the 1989 S2; that's 208 bhp without a turbocharger. What shall we do next?

By the time you read this, there will be more power, more refinements. The only way to keep a Porsche book up-to-date would be to make it loose-leaf, with (say) yearly or even six-monthly updates. If you already have a Porsche, you will know about the anti-lock braking; the airbags for both the driver and the passenger; and the appearance (at long last!) of a drophead or Cabriolet body for the S2 though not (at the time of writing) for the sohc models, whether normally aspirated or turbocharged. If you don't already have a Porsche, dream on. Maybe one day . . .

TRACK

otor racing is different things to different people. To some, who are perhaps the 'mainline' addicts, racing is the drive itself: the relentless concentration, the razor's edge between elation and death. At the other end of the spectrum it is a spectator sport; or more than just 'spectator', for that implies that it is only seen, and a motor race is also an unforgettable kaleidoscope of sounds and smells and even the taste of dust in the throat. Somewhere between these extremes there are the engineers, the tuners, the sponsors; those who know that they will never be the stars, but who still want to be nearer the cars than the other side of the fence. And, of course, racing is a proving ground and (if you can win!) the finest form of advertising that a sporting vehicle manufacturer could wish for.

From their inception Porsches were sports/racing oriented. To anyone who is less than, say, 40 years old, it may be hard to believe that once upon a time, young men (and the occasional young woman) would drive their road cars to the track, tape the headlights in case of breakage and then race in world-class events such as Le Mans or the Targa Florio. Since the 1950s, racing cars have become so specialized – and so fast – that they could hardly be made street-legal. Also, racing drivers have changed greatly. At one time they were mostly independently wealthy young men who raced for the fun of it, using their own money unless or until they were good enough to drive for a major manufacturer's team. With increasing affluence, and access to motor cars, the sport

has become very much more democratic.

The history of Porsche cars, the ones that have born the *Herr Professor Doktor Doktor*'s name, has neatly spanned that period in which even 'sports-racing' cars have become almost unrecognizably different from their road-going stablemates; and Porsche cars have exemplified the pattern of evolution.

It would be impossible to list all of Porsche's victories, even if we confined ourselves only to major races. Somewhere in Stuttgart, or Zuffenhausen, or Weissach, if they keep such records, there must be whole ledgers recording Porsche triumphs. As with the rest of this book, we have room only for the triumphs.

The first victory was modest enough, a class win in a round-the-houses race at Innsbruck on 11 July, 1948. It would be eminently forgettable if it were not for the car

ABOVE *The first appearance of the 356 cars at Le Mans. This is the lightmetal Gmünd Coupe driven by August Veuillet, the French importer of the day. He was partnered by Edmonde Mouche. They won the 1100cc class with an average speed of 140 kph (87.5 mph).*

PORSCHE

which won it: 356/1, the very first of all Porsches. They started as they meant to go on, with success after success.

Unlike, say, General Motors (which almost killed the Corvette with a steadfast refusal to countenance racing in any form), Porsche not only believed in the old saying that 'racing improves the breed'; the management stood for the principle *in person*. That original 356/1 victory was at the hands of Herbert Kaes, Ferry Porsche's nephew; that's how much they believe in racing. As well as works entries, they have always been willing to sell racers to *privateers*, and the Porsche name has arguably been glorified as much by amateurs as by works team drivers.

At first there were not many events in which to enter the new cars. In a war-devastated Europe, few could afford such luxuries. As early as 1950, though, the same type of driver that had raced before the war was racing again. At the 1950 Midnight Sun Rally in Sweden, Prince Joachim zu Furstenberg and his co-driver Count Constantin Berckheim won the 1100cc class, and the Countess Cecilia Koskull took the ladies' award in a Gmünd coupé. Count von der Muhle-Eckhart and Rudolf Sauerwein won their class, and came second overall, at the Interlaken

International Rally. And Otto Mathé won the 1100 class in the Alpine Rally. At that time there were fewer than 50 Porsches on the road, and the racers used Volkswagen engines with a reduced bore (73.5 instead of 75mm) to get them under the 1100cc limit; the regular engine was of course 1131cc.

The first works entry was, appropriately enough, at Le Mans in 1951. Of course, they won their class (750–1100cc), and they were 20th overall. Replicas of the Le Mans racer were then catalogued for general sale as the 356SL!

At Baden-Baden in the same year three cars with the new 1300 engine were entered privately by Prince zu Leiningen, Count Berckheim and Richard von Frankenberg. They averaged 75 mph (120 kph) for 30 hours, with a fuel consumption of 24 mpg (Imperial – 20 mpg American), which would be all but impossible to equal today. At Travemünde, Count Berckheim won his class in the 1951 rally; Picard and Farge took their class (and came fourth overall) at the Tour de France.

At the Liège-Rome-Liège Rally, Count von der Mühle and Paul von Guilleaume took the 1500 class win with another new engine and finished third overall. And this was just one year in Porsche's racing history!

To make life still more interesting, Porsche tried to win a few records in September 1951. They used three cars; an 1100 and two 1500s.

The 1100, with a 62 bhp alcohol-burning engine, took the class records for 500 miles (at 100.3 mph), 1000 km (at 101.4 mph) and 6 hours (at 101.1 mph, 606.6 miles total).

The open 1500 took the same records for its class, but (of course) faster: 500 miles at 116.6 mph, 1000 km at 115.3 mph, and 6 hours at 114.35 mph (686.1 miles total).

The highly streamlined ex-Le Mans 1500 was after the Class F record (up to 1500cc)

BELOW *Jose Herrarte seen in his Porsche Typ 550 Spider during the 1953 Carrera Panamericana, Mexico.*

for 72 hours. On the third day of non-stop driving, they lost first, second and fourth gears; but even so, they completed the full 72 hours at an average speed of 94.66 mph, a total of 6,815.5 miles (10,904.8 km). This was very roughly equivalent to driving from Los Angeles to New York and back in three days! Not only was it a new class record; it was also a new world record.

With the exception of the gearbox problem, this stunt demonstrated a truth which was to hold good ever after. There might be faster cars than a Porsche, and there might well be cars that handled better; but there were very, very few cars which were even as reliable as a Porsche, and none that was more reliable.

OPPOSITE *Main picture: This photo taken at the 1988 Mille Miglia shows two Porsche's 550's. The white one is an RS of 1955 and the red car is a series A RS of 1957.*

OPPOSITE, INSETS TOP AND BELOW *A Porsche 550 RS tackles the small slope and tight left hander into the square at Marostica during the 1988 Mille Miglia.*

In 1952, Count Berckheim and Count Lurani entered a Gmünd coupé for the Mille Miglia, the gruelling 'Thousand Miles' through the length of Italy; and, as usual, they won their class. They also had trouble with the gearbox, though: their car was race-prepared to the max, complete with the legendary Fuhrman cam, and delivered 70 bhp, which was more than twice what the Volkswagen box had been designed to handle.

Le Man was a relative failure; they only won the 1100 class, because the lone 1500 that was entered (Lachaize/Martin) was disqualified in the 19th hour because the driver did not switch off during refuelling, and the other 1100 (von Hanstein/Muller) suffered from a crumbly gearbox. Of course, most manufacturers would have considered a class win a success. At the Liège-Rome-Liège, Porches were first, third and fourth.

In addition to sports-car racing on road and track, Porsches also did well in hillclimbs; in 1952, for example, Porsche took eight out of ten class placings on the Ballon d'Alsace, and in October of the previous year Max Hoffman had taken class honour across the pond, at a hillclimb at Mount Equinox, Vermont.

At California's Pebble Beach in April 1952 two 356SLs were less than successful because of brake problems, but after the owner (John von Neumann) pulled the top off the Gmünd coupé and fitted a tonneau (to prevent turbulence), there was very little that could beat it in the 1.5 litre class.

This was around the time that the true sports-racer was on the way out, though: the days of the drive-to-the-shops, drive-to-the-track, drive-*on*-the-track, and drive home were numbered. The HRDs, Healys, TRs, MGs, Morgans and even the DB2s and XK120s were just not competitive with the new cars, which were specially built for the track and carried the bare minimum of necessities to qualify legally as 'road' cars: a vestigial passenger seat, luggage space and the like. All of the above cars could, like the 356, be mightily breathed upon to make them go faster, and several companies maintained competition

departments to do just that: the 356SL was an example.

One of the new generation of 'specials' builders was Walter Glöckler from Frankfurt. His first and second specials were mid-engined, Porsche-powered; he was so successful with the first, winning the German 1100cc championship in 1950, that Porsche started giving him factory support. In return, he started calling his cars Porsches. The third Glöckler Porsche, based on a shortened 356 pan, was rear-engined, but the fourth reverted to mid-engine layout and was actually displayed as a Porsche at both Geneva and Frankfurt in 1953; and encouraged by the reception of this vehicle, Ferry authorized an all-Porsche racer, car type 550 with engine type 547.

The 550 was a simple ladder-type chassis, based on the early Glöcklers, with the engine rotated about the rear axle like the original 356/1, even down to the 'leading arm' suspension. Until the Type 547 engine was available, the cars used the 1500 Super roller-bearing engine, delivering about 80 bhp.

The new car won – one is tempted to say 'of course' – at its first outing, at the 'Ring on 31 May, 1953. For Le Mans, two 550s were fitted with low roofs which probably did less for streamlining than they did for restricting visibility and overheating the drivers. The two cars were first and second in their class (1500cc) and fifteenth and sixteenth overall, crossing the finish line in the same sequence, and at the same distance apart, as they had started.

At the end of the season, both prototypes were sold to Jarolslav Juhan, who entered them in a race which ran the length of Mexico, across appalling roads in extremes of temperature: the Carrera Panamericana. It was as a result of the class win by one of these cars that the model name 'Carrera' entered the Porsche vocabulary.

Even before these semi-obsolete cars immortalized a race that would otherwise have been almost completely forgotten by now, another 550 appeared at the 'Ring in

August 1953; and this time, the 547 engine was ready.

It was an extraordinary contrivance. The four overhead cams (two on each bank) had a shaft-and-spur drive of unbelievable complexity, with a central drive shaft below the crankshaft and then on each side a shaft to the middle of the heads driven by bevel gears. At the outboard ends of these shafts,

more bevel gears drove the camshafts. The heads were twin-plugged as a concession to the still generally abysmal fuel that was available, and according to Fuhrmann it took eight hours to time the engine under ideal conditions, or maybe twice as long if the tolerances were not perfect. This was the engine which prompted factory jokes about hiring an asbestos octopus to change the plugs, and where many people found it easier to drop out the engine to work on it rather than trying to do anything *in situ*.

It did however deliver 110 bhp even in its initial form, and the 550 into which it was fitted was redesigned somewhat to put the suspension back in 'normal' trim, ie trailing instead of leading arms. In the 1954 Mille Miglia, it took class honours (Hans Hermann at the wheel, with Herbert Linge as mechanic)

a small-bore Type 547), but both did it somewhat by default; two 1500s dropped out with holed pistons, and the one that did finish (the only vehicle in its class to do so) crossed the line on three cylinders, while the 1100 was the only survivor in *its* class. In the 1954 Carrera Panamericana, the last to be held, the 547-engined 550s were first and second in their class and third and fourth overall.

ABOVE *A view of the Porsche box during the 1956 Le Mans race. On the right is Ferry Porsche.*

and it was sixth overall. This was quite an achievement in a field which included such massive (and well-funded) exotica as 300SLR Mercedes, Aston Martins, Jaguars and more, all of which had very much larger engines and more substantial construction than the little Porsche.

At Le Mans, matters were less successful. True, the Porsches both won the 1500 and the 1100 classes (one of the four cars entered had

The 550/1500RS now became catalogued cars, but to simplify the plethora of numbers and letters, they were sold as Spyders. Only two were sold in 1954, but 63 were sold in 1955 and another 13 in 1956. Although these were now more racing cars than sports cars, they could still be driven on the public road; this was the car that James Dean was driving when he died, apparently disbelieving to the last that the other driver had not seen him. At

the 1955 Le Mans, scene of far worse carnage, the Porsches finished first and second in both the 1100 and 1500 classes and took the Index of Performance for the first time; hitherto, this had been pretty much a French preserve.

The 550 was a tricky car to drive, in the great Porsche tradition. Where speed or reliability was at a premium, little could touch it; but over shorter distances or more twisted

ABOVE *Umberto Maglioli in the new Type 718 RSK of 1957, seen during tests for the 1000Km's at the Nürburgring.*

BELOW *Nurburgring 1957, 1000Km's, testing of the new Typ 718 RSK. In the cockpit is Herbert Linge.*

circuits, Lotus and Cooper were nimbler. For 1956, therefore, a new space-frame 550A appeared with three times the torsional stiffness, five times the beam stiffness, and a new rear suspension which removed the tendency of the earlier car to execute (or attempt to execute) such balletic manoeuvres as a *cabriole* on bumps or a *grand jetté* on corners.

The initial showing of the 550A in 1956 was not particularly impressive; at the Mille Miglia, it retired. At the 'Ring, it put up a more promising fourth in the 1000 km at the hands of Wolfgang von Trips and Umberto Maglioli, while a private Swiss entrant (Michael May) foreshadowed an as-yet distant controversy by fitting his car with an aerofoil over the cockpit. Feathering the wing for the straights, but angling it down for the corners, he lapped faster than the works cars in practice. This innovation was promptly banned.

The breakthrough came at the Targa Florio, though, the incredibly punishing road-

race around the roads of Sicily. Only one car was entered, and it faced stiff competition from a 300S Maserati and a Monza Ferrari; but it won. It was not just a class win: it was an outright, first-past-the-post, nobody-else-went-faster win. The class win at Le Mans a little later in the year, and the fifth place overall, was almost an anticlimax.

Various types of 550A, some street-legal and others not, competed for years to come; they were still getting class wins in the early 1960s. One famous 550A, though, was 'Mickey Mouse', a smaller, lighter car with a magnesium body which was noteworthy for two reasons. One of them was the terrifying accident at the Avus circuit in 1956, when von Frankenberg had a mishap on the banking, flew the car for a considerable distance, complete with at least one somersault, but managed to survive without serious injury. The car is also significant because it inspired the Type 718 or RSK. Unfortunately, a crash

eliminated the RSK at Le Mans in 1957, and both works 550As retired (one by running out of fuel!) but a privately-entered American-owned 550A (Hugus/de Beaufort) still took the class award.

Larger versions of the 547 engine also followed: 1587cc for the 1600 hillclimb class, 1697cc for the corresponding 2-litre class. At Buenos Aires, the first major race of the 1958 season, the RSK was not ready but a 1600-engined 550A came in fourth; the drivers were Jean Behra and Stirling Moss. Behra also brought home a second in the Targa Florio

BELOW AND BOTTOM *The Porsche Spyder RS60 of 1959, brought the company its greatest success up to that time. Familiar with long distance racing which included an overall win in the 12 hour Sebring race.*

and third overall at Le Mans, taking the 2-litre class with a 1600cc motor car and beating everything but the big boys who had almost twice the engine capacity! Another Porsche, the Barth/Frere 1500, came in fourth with (of course) a class win in their capacity.

With the team involved in Formula 1 racing, 1959 was not a promising year for the works sports-racers. Le Mans was a fiasco: of six Porsche entries, none finished. At Avus, Behra had a fatal argument with a concrete bollard, but Count Carel Godin de Beaufort had a luckier escape: after flying over the banking, he found himself right-way-up in the paddock, so he simply drove out to rejoin the fun. On a more successful note, Barth and Seidel did, however, manage to win the Targa Florio again. *Privateers* continued to win everywhere; in RSKs, 550As, 550s and even 356s.

For the 1960 season, the *gentils organizateurs* or motor-racing decided that they would make an attempt to turn the clock back a little, and require cars that bore a

greater resemblance to something that might actually be driven on the road: wider cockpits, bigger windshields, and space for a suitcase. With a four-inch-longer wheelbase (which also improved the handling) and the revised body shape, the RSK became the R60 – a car which brought an overall first at Sebring (Gendebien/Hermann), and yet another outright win at the Targa Florio (Bonnier/ Hermann), even if the works experience at Le Mans was little short of disastrous: the Barth/ Seidel R60 finished 11th with only two gears left, while a second works car retired with a thrown rod and a third with a cracked piston. A works Carrera did however finish sixth overall (and first in class, naturally), driven by Linge and Walter.

In 1961, the RS60 became an RS61 with very little change. The Sports Car Club of America saw R61s clean up the E class, and Porsche also built two special hard-top RS61s and a pretty little Spyder with a wheelbase lengthened by four inches. Unfortunately, the Targa Florio went to a Ferrari (albeit a Ferrari

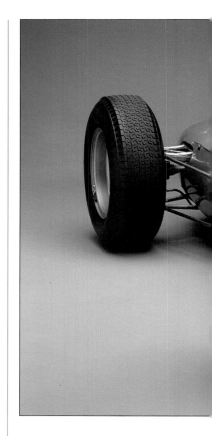

ABOVE AND BELOW *The Porsche Formula 1 car of 1962 used an 8 cylinder, air cooled, opposed piston engine. Raced by Dan Gurney, it won the French Grand Prix and then Solitude. After this the company withdrew from Grand Prix racing.*

with a rear engine!) though the W-RS came second. All three of the RS61/718 variants were entered at Le Mans, with plain-bearing 547-type engines, and the W-RS took fifth overall and first in the 2-litre class; but Formula 1 and GT racing was absorbing more and more of Porsche's interest.

The GT class was tailor-made for Porsche, a whole class which attempted to preserve the original spirit of sports-racing, but even here the rules were being stretched to the limits, and Porsche were among the most enthusiastic stretchers.

The Carrera, as we have already seen in Chapter 3, was a Type 347 engine in a 356 body. The trick was first tried for the Liège-Rome-Liège run in 1954, with a Type 547 in a Gmund body, but then a run of 'homologation specials' was conceived; and, as seems to happen with Porsche homologation specials, there was such a demand that they ended up making far more than were required merely for certification as a production car. Regular class winners, and occasional outright

ABOVE AND LEFT *With strong opposition from such names as Lotus, Cooper and Ferrari, the Porsche Formula 2 race car managed to capture the desirable 'Coupes des constructeurs' in 1960. This is the type 718/2 Formula 2 race car.*

winners, they were *the* car to be reckoned with in such events as the Liège-Rome-Liège, the Tour de France, the Alpine Rally and the Mille Miglia. The ultimate GT cars, the Abarth Carrera and the 2000GS/GT, have already been covered in Chapter 3.

Of the single-seater campaigns, the less said the better. From 1957 to 1962, Porsche pursued both Formula 2 (under 1500cc, running on pump fuel) and Formula 1 (for the 1961 season, announced in 1958, also under 1500cc). The 718/2 (Version 2 of the 718 racer) was not disastrous – indeed, there were some notable victories such as the first, second and third at Aintree in 1960 and second, third, fourth and fifth at Solitude in the same year, with a Constructors' Championship. Although no new cars were ready for the Formula 1-season of 1961, the 1½ litre flat 8 (!) in the Type 804 space-frame entered seven World Championship events in 1962 and scored a first, a third, a fifth, a sixth, a seventh and a ninth. In 1962, though, Porsche had the sense to see that Colin Chapman's monocoque Lotus 25 completely outclassed any space-frame car, and an era had passed. Wisely, they pulled out of single seaters.

In 1963, Ferry decided that a new sports/racer, again with the emphasis on the racer, was in order; and thus was born the 904. It was initially intended to have the new flat-6 from the 911, but this was not ready; and so the long-suffering 547 was mated to the new 5-speed transmission which *was* ready. The chassis reverted to a ladder, the first such chassis design in a Porsche since the original 550, and the exceptionally sleek and rather lovely body was designed by Butzi and made by Heinkel out of GRP; it was bonded to the chassis for extra strength.

In March 1964, the 904 took a modest enough ninth at the Sebring circuit, its first race, but then – only a month later – it won the Targa Florio, the fifth time a Porsche had done so. Usually, no-one remembers who finished second; but when the Linge/Balzarini 904 took second place after the Pucci/Davis

RIGHT, BELOW AND BOTTOM *1964 saw the 904 GTS Carrera Coupe. The car was designed by Ferdinand Alexander Porsche (Butzi) and was the first Porsche to have a plastic body. Fitted with 4, 6 and 8 cylinder engines it was one of the most successful race sports cars of the early sixties.*

904, people remembered. It looked as though Porsche might have another long-term winner on their hands. The car also did well at Spa, Rheims and the 'Ring, and although the works 904s both retired at Le Mans, *privateers* came in 7th, 8th, 10th, 11th and 12th. Paradoxically, *privateer* successes enhanced the Porsche reputation almost more than a works win would have done, for the works cars were 904/8s with the flat-8 Formula 1 engine, while the cars that finished were regular, 'over-the-counter' cars. On the other hand, the 904/8s were clocked at 175 mph on the Mulsanne straight. A twin-plugged 904/6 also made a brief (but unsuccessful) appearance; this was of course a 904 with a variant of the originally-planned flat-6 engine. Regardless of engine variation, the 904 won the 2 litre GT championship that year.

Some people will try to tell you that the 904 was the ultimate Porsche road car; the 'last of the sports racers.' With all due respect, it is unlikely that any of these boasters has

BELOW INSET AND OVERLEAF *This is the 1966 Porsche 906 Carrera 6 Coupe. It proved unbeatable in the 2 litre sports car class using a light 210 hp six cylinder engine. Wing style doors were used for the first time by Porsche on their all plastic body (below centre).*

ever driven one, let alone tried to ride in one. For all that they are nominally road cars, the ideal passenger would be an anorexic masochist, and the 904/4 engine was not the most tractable or easily maintained unit in the world. Besides, if you want the ultimate roadgoing Porsche, do not forget that there is at least one street-legal 917. It is just as cramped and inconvenient as the 904/4, but it is even more beautiful (in its own bizarre way), and a very great deal faster. It all depends on what you are prepared to put up with in your search for the ultimate!

Even so, the 904 achieved a second in the Monte in '65 (Boringer/Wütherlich) and a third at the Targa Florio (in 904/6 form), to say nothing of the 904/6 which was fourth overall at Le Mans, where it also won the Index of Performance.

Porsche engines were also used in British Elva bodies, and the Elva-Porsche influenced Ferdinand Piëch's decision to order a minimalist, very low body on a 904/8 chassis, a

car which is derided by some as ugly but which to others carries the ultimate beauty of functionality. A gull-wing 906 followed, including several with flat-8s, still within the 2-litre limit. At Le Mans in 1966 they finished fourth, fifth, sixth, seventh and eighth. The first three cars were all Ford GT40s, another immortal design, but powered by 7-litre engines. Porsche won the Index of Performance.

Also in 1966, the (then relatively new) 911 began to show its potential as a rally car, winning the Austrian and the German rallies outright; this can hardly have been a surprise, given Porsche's performance in the Targa Florio, the Mille Miglia, and all the other road-races (which were halfway to rallies) that Porsches had won, but apparently it had not previously occurred to Porsche to stress rallying much, because they saw it as a poor man's sport. In 1967, 911s won the Tulip, the Geneva, the Osterreichring, the Polish and the Marathon de la Route, though the last was won by a 911R with all the 'added lightness' they could get (plastic and light alloy body

parts, virtually no trim, and even the cigarette lighter and ashtray removed to save an ounce or two) and a 906 type engine with about 210 bhp. The Monte fell to a 911T in 1969 and to a 911S in both 1970 and 1971.

Meanwhile, another racing Porsche had appeared, the 910. Clearly a 906 derivative, it could accept either a 911-style 6 or a Type 771 flat-8. The chassis was a space-frame, strengthened by having some of the bodywork bonded to it, though an enormous section of tail lifted to reveal the engine and a good deal of what book designers call 'working' (ie blank) space.

The success of the small-engined 910s was remarkable, given that they were competing with GT40s and Ferrari P4s, though overall firsts were less common than more modest placings: in 1967, there was a fourth at Daytona, thirds at Sebring and Monza, a second at Spa, and two firsts, one at the Targa Florio and one at the 'Ring 1000 km. At Le Mans, a 6-cylinder 910 achieved sixth overall, and the hillclimb victories were legion.

Even as the 910 was winning races though, a new car was being planned for Le Mans, the long-tailed (langheck) 907. It was not a particularly stable car (a fine Porsche tradition), but it was quick, and although the best they could do at Le Mans in 1967 was fifth

ABOVE AND LEFT
Natural favorites for hill climb racing, Porsche Spyder won more than their fair share of events. Thin plastic body panels, low windshields and an aluminium space frame contributed to enormous savings in weight. Gerhard Mitter and Rolf Stommelen were the main drivers for the 1967 and 1968 European Hillclimb Championships.

overall (with a 2-litre class win and the Index of Performance) it was not until the February 1968 races that they really proved themselves. Not only did they finish 1-2-3; they also crossed the line in line abreast. They also won the Targa Florio after losing, and then recovering, a wheel.

The CSI (the forerunner of the FIA) forced the introduction of the next racer, the 908. Apparently, with a fit of Gallic logic, or nostalgia, or mere chauvinism, they declared that prototypes would be limited to 3 litres and limited-production cars to 5 litres, with a minimum requirement of 50-off for homologation. To be charitable, maybe they were trying (once again) to return Le Mans cars to their sports-car roots; to be uncharitable, maybe they were engaging in a typical bit of French rule-rigging to give Matra and Renault more of a chance. To cap it all, they gave only six months' notice of the change, in breach of their own rules.

Whatever their reasoning, their approach was too high-handed for a number of manufacturers to stomach. Not only did Ford leave in a huff: so did Ferrari, Chaparal and Lola-Aston Martin.

Porsche hung in. They not only introduced a new car, the 908; they also introduced a new engine, a 3-litre flat 8 which was essentially a

ABOVE AND RIGHT *Featured here is the Porsche 908 Longtail Coupe. It was raced in both longtail and shortail versions. The 908 made its debut at Le Mans in 1968.*

BELOW *The engine was an 8 cylinder air-cooled opposed piston engine. It produced three hundred and fifty hp at 8400 rpm and had a capacity of 2997cc Drive was through 5 speed gearbox using a limited slip differential. Top speed was in the region of 320 kph (200 mph).*

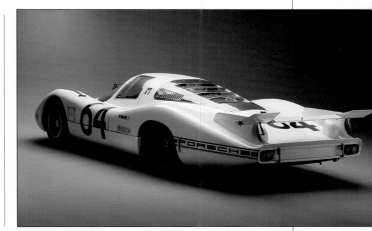

911 engine with two cylinders grafted on and chain-driven double overhead cams on both banks of cylinders; it was, in effect, a derivative of a short-lived dohc 911 engine (the 916) which had been tried and rejected in 1966-7.

Once again the car was fast but hair-raisingly unstable. Instability in a car that can do 190 mph on the Mulsanne straight is something you can do without. They were not a success at the *Grand Prix de l'Endurance*, though they did win at the 'Ring a month later with shortened tails (*kurzheck*). Further development led to modest successes in 1968, but 1969 was the year of the 908: the first three places at the BOAC 500 at Brands, the first four at the Targa Florio, and the first five

at the 'Ring. It achieved a remarkable second at Le Mans, beaten by the much larger Gulf Ford. The competition career continued too: a 908/3 won the Targa Florio in 1970, the Road Atlanta Can-Am in the same year, and the 1000 km at the 'Ring in both 1971 and 1972.

A far, far greater car was already in production, though: the mighty 917. The CSI effectively admitted that they had made a mistake with the 50-off rule for limited-production cars, and lowered the requirement for 25 in the spring of 1968. This brought Ford and Chevvy back into contention, but by now, Porsche had the bit between their teeth and reasoned that a limited run of 25 was by no means out of sight. They therefore built a bigger, stronger 908 and added four more cylinders to the 908 engine for a 4.5 litre flat-12. In reality, the engineering was a lot more complex than that – for example, the drive was taken from the middle of the engine, in order to avoid an excessively whippy crankshaft – but to the casual observer, that

*LEFT AND BELOW
Making its debut on the
22nd March, 1969 at
Sebring, the Porsche
908/02 Spyder went on to
capture the first three
places at Brands Hatch.
From six starters, four
finished in the first four
places in the Targa
Florio. The 908 brought
Porsche its first World
Championship for
makes.*

was what it looked like. Before they ever raced it, Porsche priced the car at a cool DM140,000; for a while, it was in the *Guinness Book of Records* as the most expensive production car in the world.

The CSI looked askance. Was this really a production car? Until they saw 25 of them, they were not prepared to homologate them. The story of the proof has passed into legend: on 21 April, 1969, the inspectors were shown 25 cars lined up outside the factory, and offered a box of keys to try any or all of them, to show that they were not dummies. The car had been given the go-ahead only 10 months earlier.

It was a familiar story. The car was blindingly fast – well over 200 mph (320 kph), with a minimum of about 450 bhp – but it was also a long way from an easy drive. The tyres were too narrow; the aerodynamics were not all they should have been; and the suspension offered too-great attitude changes. At Le Mans, the very first customer 917 killed its

driver, and the Elford/Attwood car had to retire, though one 917 was clocked at 236 mph (393 kph) on the Mulsanne straight, about a third of a mile a *minute* faster than anything else, ever. At the Osterreichring 1000 km, though, the car won by a handy margin, and it was clear that with some development there was going to be nothing on earth to touch the new car.

Factory team management was handed over to the Gulf-sponsored John Wyer organization, and later in 1969 the short-tailed 917 was modified with a new tail to give more downthrust.

At Daytona in 1970 the Gulf-Porsches finished first and second. Of the 24 Championship races they entered that year, Porsche won no fewer than 15 in 917s and four in 908s, which did not leave much for anyone else; and at last, at last, there was the outright first at Le Mans, albeit under the Porsche-Salzburg banner after all three of the Gulf cars (and one of the Porsche-Salzburg cars) had dropped out.

TOP *Porsche number 40 the 908/03 Spyder driven by Kinnunen and Rodriguez to victory at the 1970 Targa Florio.*

ABOVE LEFT *Joe Siffert driving another 908/03 in the 1970 Targa Florio.*

ABOVE RIGHT *Siffert and Redman celebrate at 1970 Targe Florio.*

The flat-16 that was designed for the 1971 season was never needed, because Ferrari opted to stay in the 3-litre prototype class, so the 12s from Zuffenhausen ruled the roost. Alfa's T33/3s won at Brands, Watkins Glen and the Targa Florio, but Porsche triumphed at Buenos Aires, Daytona, and (most importantly) Le Mans; a Gulf Porsche came in first, and a Martini Porsche (Salzburg had found a new sponsor) was second.

The Pink Pig, one of the more whimsical Porsche 917 models, unfortunately ran out of

TOP LEFT *12 Cylinder Boxer engine fitted to the 917 Race Coupe, winner of the 1970 and '71 World Championship for makes.*

TOP RIGHT *The 1970 917 Short Tail Coupe.*

ABOVE AND RIGHT
The Porsche 917 of Hans Herman and Dick Attwood during the 1970 Le Mans 24 Hour Race. This was Porsche's first overall victory at Le Mans.

breath and turned its trotters up before the end of the race.

Early in the 1970s, Porsche also went for the Can-Am in a big way, but despite 660 bhp in the 917/10 (from 5347cc), the McLaren/ Chevvys were even more powerful at 780 bhp, and brute power won the day. The answer was obvious to Porsche; it was something they had done often enough before. They needed more power, so they turbocharged the car.

The dynamometer showed peak readings of 1000 bhp, and to make sure that the power stayed on the deck (there was a risk of spinning the inside wheel on corners), they simply removed the differential. Archie Frazer-Nash would have been proud of them. They took the championship easily in 1972, but the 1973 917/30 delivered a *regular* 1100 bhp, with peak or 'flash' readings of 1500 bhp.

There was no contest; it was like racing a 911 against bicycles. Their victory was so totally convincing that the rules were changed to exclude the Porsches, not *de jure* but *de facto*. Maybe there were French Canadians on the board, or maybe it was just the US motor industry, which had already begun its long slide, but Porsche quit, very much while they were ahead.

TOP *Main picture Porsche's racing credentials are used to boost roadgoing sales and image.*

INSET *Triumphant Porsches seen during the 1971 Daytona Race.*

OVERLEAF *The most photographed race car of the 1971 Le Mans race, the Porsche 917/20 Coupe with its most unusual paint work. Driven by Joest and Kauhsen who held fifth place until the car left the track causing heavy damage after sustaining breaking problems. Finally the 'Pig' ended up with trotters in the air.*

Thereafter, the people at Porsche were at something of a loss. They had produced a world beater. What next?

The answer, as it turned out, was rather like the answer had been a decade or more earlier: why not race something that was a bit closer to the roadgoing cars? A go-faster 911, for instance?

The 911 had already been raced (as distinct from rallied) successfully. As early as 1967, a privately-entered 911S had come second in the GT class at Le Mans, and by 1972, John Fitzpatrick had walked away with the European GT Championship.

The 'base' 911, as far as racing was concerned, was the Carrera RS 2.7, as already described in Chapter 5. The RSR was an RS with the engine taken out still further (to 2806cc), twin-plugged heads and other engine modifications (including a massive oil cooler in the nose), and tyres that looked a yard wide but were only 9 inches at the front and 11 inches at the rear; with 300 bhp at 8000 rpm, the big, sticky tyres were a necessity.

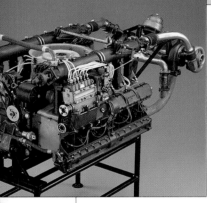

Even before it was homologated, it won
the 1973 Daytona 24-hours outright, running
in the prototype class; shortly thereafter, they
went to 2994cc and 315 bhp, with 10.5 inch
wheels at the front and 15 inch wheels at the
back, with a vast rear spoiler. It was in this
form that a 911 won the very last Targa Florio;
a fitting end to the race, one of the last great
road races. Porsche themselves never raced
these spectacular machines; they just sold
them to people who wanted to race – and the
people who wanted to race also found that
their RSRs tended to win.

For 1974, another few bhp were found
cowering inside the engine of the RSR 3.0, and
when they were dragged out into the light,
there were 330 bhp on tap. *Privateers* won
the IMSA championship, the International
Race of Champions, the European GT
championship, the FIA GT cup and any other
number of major and minor events; and then,
in 1975, they simply did the same again.

The engine was approaching its limits in
normally aspirated form, but Porsche
unconcernedly turbocharged it for 1974,
bringing the capacity down to 2.14 litres:
under FIA rules, this was considered the
equivalent of a 3-litre unblown car. There
were around 450 bhp available from the flat
6, and the rear wheels really were almost
half a yard wide, at 17 inches. Unfortunately,
steering and gearbox problems held the Turbo
Carrera down to second place at Le Mans; the
same car also achieved a second at Watkins
Glen, but never a first in the one season that it
was raced.

For the 1975 season, the RSRs continued
on their own sweet way, and the 2.14 Turbo
engine appeared in Reinhold Jöst's 908/03,
where it did well, but not well enough – the
best showing was a second at Monza. With an
unblown 3-litre engine, the same car came
fourth overall at Le Mans.

It was the 1976 season which saw the next
big changes. The groups for that year were
Group 3 (production touring cars), Group 4
(limited-production touring cars), Group 5
(World Championship of Makes, a semi-
'silhouette' formula for modified production
cars) and Group 6 (3-litre prototypes).

Porsche contested Groups 4, 5 and 6 with
the 930-based 934, 935 and 936. The 934, the
'baby' of the class, was very fully equipped,
even down to the electric windows; that was

the only way to bring it up to the minimum weight requirements! It still boasted 485 bhp (with more available at minimal effort) from its turbocharged 3-litre engine, equivalent to an unblown 4.2 litre under the 1.4x equivalency rules. There were several under-the-skin changes, such as a water-air intercooler and a repositioned cooling fan, but it was still quite close to stock.

The 935 aimed for the 4-litre class, with a 2856cc engine (remember the equivalency factor) and an official rating of 590 bhp. It embodied such exotic features as titanium coil springs all round, and a body made of a glass fibre/polyurethane sandwich, but the floor pan was straight off the 911 production line. It had to be ballasted to bring it up to the minimum weight.

Finally, the 936 bore almost no resemblance to a 911/930, with a space-frame, the turbo 2.14 engine, and a body which owed a great deal to the 917.

At the 'Ring, a stretched throttle cable (of all ridiculous faults!) relegated the 936 to fifth place; but that first race was not an omen. The 936 won everything else that it entered that year, most notably at Le Mans where a 936

TOP AND ABOVE *The 911 Carrera RSR Turbo 2.1. In 1974 the 6 cylinder engine of the 911 was given additional power via turbo charging. (Previously restricted to the 917/30 CamAm race sports car). This now increased the output of this 2.1 litre 6 to 500 hp.*

ABOVE RIGHT *Shown at Daytona in February 1973 is the group 5 2.8 Carrera RSR of Gregg and Hayward.*

was first overall; a 935 dominated Group 5; a 934 did the same for Group 4; and a Carrera won the IMSA category.

For the 1977 season, changes were comparatively minor, though the 936 grew twin blowers instead of one. Porsche won every single round of the World Championship of Makes, every round of the Can-Am series, and 7 out of 14 rounds of the IMSA Camel GT championship. A 936 won at Le Mans, albeit running on five cylinders with one piston holed, and the 935 and the 934 took their groups as well. Porsche also discovered that there is such a thing as being too successful.

Because motor racing was becoming a Porsche advertising exercise, rather than a genuine contest (at least in the eyes of the

RIGHT *Winner of the 1976 World Championship for Makes Porsche 935 Coupe.*

ABOVE *The 1976 World Championship Team: from the left Manfred Schurti, Rolf Stommelen, race boss Manfred Jantke, Jochen Mass and Jacky Ickx.*

press), the struggle between Ford and BMW in the 2-litre class provided a lot more excitement; you didn't know in advance who was going to win. Until, of course, Porsche decided to do so.

The 935/2 was a blown 1.4 litre 6, delivering 370 bhp. Although it overheated at its first race, this problem was quickly solved and at Hockenheim it wiped the floor with both Ford and BMW. Having made the point that Porsches could win wherever they chose to do so, the company then made the point that racing dinky little motor cars like this was beneath them, and therefore they did not bother to compete again.

In 1978, the 935 lost most of its 911 ancestry when a close reading of the regulations (a Porsche specialty) led to a tubular frame and a glass-fibre floor, which lowered the whole car by three inches. The bodywork, drawing on lessons learned from the 1.4 litre car, was also revised to give a

peculiar hump-backed look which led to the nickname 'Moby Dick'.

Under Moby Dick's skin, though, was a 4-valve-per-cylinder head, which was not only water-cooled but also electron-beam welded to the block. Camshaft drive was by gears. The capacities were 3211cc for Group 5, 2140cc for Group 6 and 2650cc for Indianapolis. In the event, the Indianapolis car never raced; the Americans took a leaf from the French book, and rewrote the rules to suit their own dinosaurs in order to avoid being humiliated on their home turf.

With the 321cc engine (4.5 litres equivalence), Moby Dick won the Silverstone in 6 hours in early 1978 but developed an oil leak at Le Mans and finished eighth overall; Porsche had to be content with second and third behind a Renault.

The following year, though, it looked as though Renault might again be in contention; so Porsche entered two works 936s, though it was a 935 which won overall (Ludwig/Wittington), with two other 935s second and third. The second place team included Paul Newman. In fourth place was a 934, which (not surprisingly) won Group 4.

The 1980 Le Mans – which was fast becoming *the* race by which Porsches were judged in a given year – was contested by three works 924 Carrera GTPs, running at almost twice the standard boost (1.3 atmospheres instead of 0.7), but they were running as prototypes and managed only sixth, twelfth and thirteenth positions. The highest-placed Porsche was second, a replica

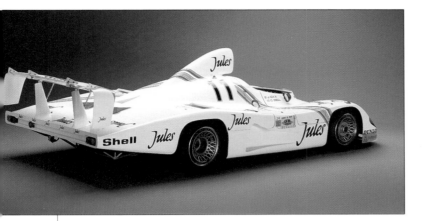

936/77 built by Reinhold Jöst and driven by Jöst and Ickx.

The following season saw Ickx and Bell win in a 936 with the Indy engine; the old 3-litre limit had been abolished, and Porsche never had any aversion to extra swept volume. The other works 936 had problems, but the Ickx/Bell car won by four complete laps after leading for the whole of the race. A 924 Carrera with a 944 turbo engine finished seventh; unfortunately, the last of the 917s, a brand new car built especially for the race for Erwin Kremer, dropped out about a third of the way through the race.

The 1982 season has already been touched upon in the Introduction – it was an unforgettable experience for anyone who was there – but the technical specifications of the cars were not mentioned. Under the new rules, Group A, Group B and Group N were production cars, while Group C replaced the old Groups 5 and 6 and was essentially a fuel-

TOP LEFT *1981 Porsche 936/81 Spyder.*

TOP RIGHT *1977 Porsche 936/77 Spyder.*

BOTTOM *1977 935/2.0 Coupe 'Baby'.*

economy formula, a field in which Porsche felt they were well placed.

They built a monocoque with a development of the Indy engine giving about 620 bhp, and called it the 956.

After finding that the car was not quite as economical as they had hoped at Silverstone, they made a few changes and entered a team of three at Le Mans. Not only did the cars roll home in team formation; they were also followed by a brace of 935s for a clean sweep from first to fifth.

The story for the next couple of years is quickly summarized. At the 1983 Le Mans, 956s filled nine of the ten first places. The winner was Al Holbert, partnered by Vern Schuppan and Hurley Haywood, and their car ran the last 8½ miles with no cylinder head coolant, and a *seriously* cooked motor. The Makes Championship went to Porsche that year, with 100 points as against 32 for Lancia, their nearest competitors.

With *no* works cars at Le Mans in 1984, *privateer* 956s were left to contest the race. Team Jöst won (Pescarolo/Ludwig), and Porsches filled eight of the first ten places. It was getting monotonous again.

There was, however, a new car for 1984, the 962. A derivative of the 956, it had a longer wheelbase (by 12cm, almost 5 ins), largely to meet the new FIA rule that the driver's feet had to be behind the front suspension, and appropriately revised bodywork. The engine

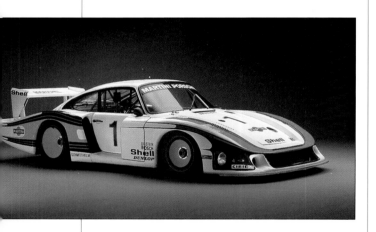

was a relatively low-tech device with a single turbocharger, single plugs, and only two valves per cylinder.

Despite the attractions of the 962, Le Mans 1985 was won *by the same car* that had won the previous year, with another *privateer* 956 second and a works 962 third. While all this was going on, though, Porsche were also involved in rallying *and* Formula 1.

LEFT *The most potent version of the 6 cylinder racing engine to date carried water cooled cylinder heads with 4 valves atop its aircooled cylinders for the first time. This is the 1978 935 'Moby Dick' Coupe.*

RIGHT AND BOTTOM *This prototype of the future Porsche 944 was raced at Le Mans under the name of 'Porsche 924 GTP Le Mans'. There was no way that the Barth/Rohrl car was going to win the 1981 Le Mans race, but a seventh place overall was certainly an achievement.*

The rally car was predictably the 911, in which Jacky Ickx had won the Paris–Dakar in 1983. For the same rally in 1984 Porsche prepared a semi-works team of four-wheel-drive 911SCs, one of which won (René Metge), though Ickx was only sixth. The back-up car, driven by a couple of factory mechanics, managed to win two of the stages in its own right!

They were not successful in 1985 but for 1986 they managed 1st, 2nd and 6th with twin-turbo, four-wheel-drive 961s – the racing version of the 959 – and they have enjoyed many other rally successes since; but it is still hard not to believe that Porsche sees rallying as a 'poor man's sport'.

The return to Formula 1 was not as car constructors, but as engine builders. The engine, introduced in 1983 to power McLarens, was an 80° twin-turbo V6 of 1499cc, with a magnesium block and titanium con-rods as well as the obvious four valves per cylinder and two cams per block. The 150 kg

(330 lb) power unit delivered 650 bhp at something over 10,000 rpm. In the first year, McLaren and Porsche were learning to work together, but in 1984 they won 12 out of 16 Grands Prix. Results in 1985 were not quite as good – Ferrari and Lotus were both in contention at times – but Porsche still won the championship, mostly as a result of greatly superior reliability.

For the 1986 season, Honda were embarrassingly good, but Alain Prost managed to clock up 72 points in his McLaren-Porsche, as against Nigel Mansell's 70 points in the Williams-Honda, though as a team the Williams-Hondas gathered the most points.

In the 1987 season, Porsche very wisely decided to pull out, leaving Honda as the engine to beat.

Meanwhile, the sports/racers continued to turn in excellent results: at the 1986 Daytona, for example, Porsche 962s came in first, second and third, in the finest Porsche tradition. On the other hand, the writing was

on the wall: a 16-race winning streak in the Camel GT ended when a Corvette GTP and a Buick Hawk GTP *both* came in ahead of the first Porsche, a 962.

Officially, though, Porsche's racing programme in 1986 was 'for technical development'; they could afford to do this, because *privateers* kept winning for them! The factory-raced 961 development of the 959 offered 680 bhp, with twin turbos, allowing top speeds well in excess of 200 mph, however, at Le Mans it was 962s that took first and second, with a 956 third; the 961 was 7th. This was Porsche's sixth consecutive Le Mans win.

LEFT AND BELOW This 956 is the first Porsche race car with a monocoque chassis and ground effects. These cars produced a sensational 1-2-3 victory at Le Mans in 1982 (above), extending their string of victories to 1983, 1984 and 1985.

RIGHT Installed in the 956 was the four stroke 6 cylinder Boxer engine with 2 exhaust turbo-chargers and inter cooler producing 620 hp at 8200 rpm from a displacement of 2649cc. Top speed was above 350 kph (218 mph).

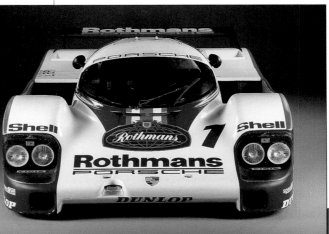

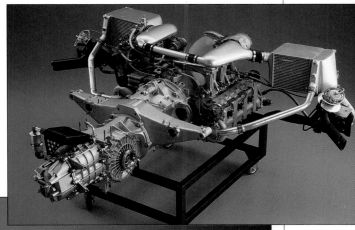

At Daytona in 1987, six 962s took the first six places, five of them with the Andial 3-litre engine, but that was the last truly brilliant win for Porsche at the American event, because 1988 saw Jaguar in 1st and 3rd place, with 962s taking 2nd and 4th – the first time in 12 years that a Porsche did not win! This was an omen of things to come, too, because at the 1988 Le Mans the big cats took 1st and 4th, with Porsche relegated to 3rd, 5th and 6th.

Obviously, this could not be permitted; and at the 1989 Daytona, Porsches took 1st and 2nd, with a Jaguar 3rd – though it is impossible not to suggest that there was a tiny bit of luck involved, with Jaguar's failings seeming to be the whim of the gods of motor racing (Mars, perhaps? Hephaestus?) rather than any fault of the cars. And then, at a very wet 1989 Le Mans, Team Sauber took their Mercedes C9s to the first, second and fifth; at last, Mercedes was back, in a big way . . .

The most recent racing year at the time of writing was 1990 – and the season wasn't over. Porsche was winning less and less, and had contrived to lose Le Mans once again: at the French Classic, Jaguar won and Nissan came on so strongly that (in the words of America's *Road and Track* magazine) it seemed to be

ABOVE AND RIGHT *Three World Championships went to the TAG-Porsche engine (right) in Formula One. Seen here is Alain Prost at Monte Carlo in 1986 in his McLaren.*

BOTTOM *In 1986 three Porsche 959's using electronically controlled all-wheel drive captured first, second and sixth places in the Paris-Dakar rally.*

merely a question of *when* Nissan would clock up their first win – 1991 or 1992. The on-again, off-again Indy car project had been knocked on the head, partly because Porsche had not really done all that well, partly because it wasn't really Porsche's idea of motor racing, but mainly because it is almost impossible to get Europeans to take the Brickyard seriously: European and international racing is what sells cars, even to Americans.

It seemed, in fact, that in 1990 Porsche was at something of a nadir as far as world-class track competition was concerned – but that could turn around in the 1991 season, because Porsche was just about to return to Formula 1. It was impossible to believe that they would be out of contention for long.

TOP *The 1989 Indy CART racer.*

ABOVE LEFT *The 1988 1000 km race at Monza.*

ABOVE RIGHT *A view of the Porsche pit during practice of the 1990 24 hour race at Le Mans.*

When I first planned this book, the racing section was not going to be all that long. I wanted a book that was mostly about road Porsches because (after all) that is what most of us get to drive – if we are lucky. I soon realized, though, that I would only be writing half a book if I wrote about Porsche without going into the racing side in at least some depth.

For those who are fortunate enough to drive roadgoing Porsches, the racing history explains where some of that road pedigree comes from; and for those who can only dream about Porsches, perhaps the ultimate dream is to put a racing Porsche on the road. It has been done before, and it could be done again . . .

Index

Picture Credits

Porsche GmbH pp: 10–16 (top), 18 (bottom) – 21, 24 (bottom), 25 (top
and centre), 27–33, 34 (top and left), 35, 36 (bottom), 37–39, 41–42, 45
(top), 46—55, 56 (bottom), 57, 61, 64–73, 76–80, 82–83, 86–92, 94,
96–111, 112 (top left and bottom), 113, 116–122, 123 (top and bottom).
J Baker Collection pp: 8–9, 22, 24 (top), 34 (inset), 36 (top), 40, 43–44,
45 (bottom), 56 (inset and top), 58–60, 62–63, 74–75, 81, 84, 93, 95, 112
(top right), 114–115, 123 (inset).
Mercedes Benz pp: 16 (top), 18 (top)
LAT Photographic pp: 6–7
Harrah Motor Collection pp:17
Volkswagen AG pp: 25 (bottom), 26
The Federal Archive, Germany pp: 23
Trevor Wood pp: front cover, title, half-title and contents page.

The J Baker Collection would like to thank Herr Klaus Parr, Librarian at
Porsche Werke 1, for his invaluable help.